NEW·ADAM

David —
Thank you for being
my friend.

Chris

i

PHILIP·CULBERTSON

The Future of Male Spirituality

NEW·ADAM

FORTRESS PRESS ▪ MINNEAPOLIS

NEW ADAM
The Future of Masculine Spirituality

Scripture quotations, unless translated from the Hebrew by the author, are adapted from the New Revised Standard Version of the Bible, copyright © 1989 by the Division of Christian Education of the National Council of the Churches of Christ in the United States of America. Used with permission.

Chapter One originally appeared in a different version in *Saint Luke's Journal of Theology* 23 (December 1988). The excerpt from "Doing It Differently" is from *To Be of Use* by Marge Piercy (New York: Doubleday, 1973) and is reprinted by permission. The excerpt from *Rubyfruit Jungle* by Rita Mae Brown (New York: Bantam Books, 1988) is reprinted by permission of Bantam Books, a division of Bantam, Doubleday, Dell Publishing Group, Inc.

Cover design: Judy Swanson
Cover art or photo: "Wilderness" by Rockwell Kent, used courtesy of the Rockwell Kent Legacies

Library of Congress Cataloging-in-Publication Data

Culbertson, Philip Leroy, 1944–
    New Adam : the future of masculine spirituality / Philip
Culbertson.
        p.   cm.
    Includes bibliographical references.
    ISBN 0-8006-2512-9
    1. Men—Religious life.   2. Men—Psychology.   I. Title.
BV4843.C85   1992
248.8'42—dc20
                                                                91-44384
                                                                CIP

The paper used in this publication meets the minimum requirements of American National Standard for Information Sciences—Permanence of Paper for Printed Library Materials, ANSI Z329.48-1984. ∞™

Manufactured in the U.S.A.   AF 1-2512
96   95   94   93   92   1   2   3   4   5   6   7   8   9   10

To Phyllis Trible,
who taught me without knowing me.

To "The Monday Night Group,"
with whom I loved and learned.

And to my children Katie and Jacob
In the name of the generations of fathers
Who wanted something better for their children.

Contents

CONTENTS

PART TWO
Prayer, Iron John, and the White Snake

Introduction

Lord, there are lots of holes in my life. There are some in the lives of my brothers and sisters. But if you wish, we shall hold hands. We shall hold very tight, and together we shall make a fine roll of fence to adorn Paradise. Amen.

—Michel Quoist

There are holes in my life, and there are holes in your life. The human condition is one of having holes in our lives, and loving and living with those who have holes in their lives. Another part of the human condition is inheriting the holes of previous generations, or perhaps it is integrating the holes of someone else with whom we are in relationship into some misfit juncture with the holes in our own lives and occasionally being victimized by what we have inherited. This concept is a biblical one. For example, in the Gospel of Matthew (23:32), the question is raised whether we are victimized by the generations that have gone before us: "Fill up, then, the measure of your ancestors!" The context suggests that while we each have an often-tragic inheritance, we also have a choice as to whether or not that inheritance will be perpetuated.

I first met feminism twenty years ago. I am not yet sure that I know her, but we have a relationship. She teaches me how much I do not yet know as a man. The God whom I met in the midst of the emotional violence of my own divorce was God the nurturer. I know that men

1

can nurture, or at least I try to nurture my children as an expression of my masculinity. But the God I met in the midst of the emotional violence of my divorce was the nurturing God who is a woman. I was surprised. She wanted only two things from me: for me to hold her hand and for me to trust her. She didn't say go to the wilderness; she said come to the wilderness. The nurturing God is quite different from the God who said to Abraham: *Lekh Lekha*, Go out from here. That directive God, the God of Abraham, is clearly male to me, just as clearly as the nurturing God is female to me. They both love, and they are both the same God. But from then on, I knew that God was just as female as male, and that I could not really understand the fullness of God until I had submitted myself to a nurturing female God, a God whose characteristics complemented the patriarchal God I had been taught to know, but whose characteristics were all opposite of his.

In the past few decades we have begun to understand how women have been victimized by the generations that have gone before and how they have been victimized by what they have inherited in their relationships with men. Many women have become weary of this victimization and have demanded radical changes in society's expectations of and opportunities offered them. Obviously those affected by such changes include not only women, but also men in all walks of society. As men have addressed feminism, many of them have discovered that they cannot respond to women's demands for justice, equality, and opportunity without exploring radical redefinitions of how manhood and maleness are understood and lived out. Men need to understand how we respond to our inherited cultural definitions of manliness, masculinity, and male psychological, emotional, sexual, and spiritual behavior.

Our society has changed rapidly in a short time, although many would claim that the changes have not been radical enough, deep enough, or broad enough. Out of men's confusion and anger in response to women's demands, and out of men's desire to take women's demands seriously, has sprung up a new field of psycho-sociology called men's studies. Suddenly a whole library of works exists in the field, which makes for fascinating reading. These men take feminism seriously and try to figure out who they have been, who they are now, what they need, and how they understand themselves. They seek ways to continue to claim all that is good about maleness and masculinity without perpetuating violence against women.

Aspects of the feminist movement have affected the religious community. For example, we see within the church the beginnings of a broader use of inclusive language, new theologies of feminism and liberation, and greater opportunities for the ministry to and by women. Some men within the church are trying to change in order to grant women the equality, justice, and opportunity that they demand. But women's demands are sometimes refused in the church. Pope John Paul II has announced that he will never approve of the ordination of women. Inclusive language continues to meet with significant opposition at the national conventions of Protestant denominations and in the new Vatican catechism. A handful of bishops in the Episcopal church threatened to leave in response to the election of Barbara Harris as Suffragan Bishop of Massachusetts. The Vatican has issued a directive silencing theologian Matthew Fox, one of the Roman church's most vocal male supporters of women and sensitive men.

Some critics would call this whole affair the war between the sexes, a war between men and women. That characterization seems terribly unfair, for many men take women's issues very seriously, just as more and more women are beginning to take sensitive men's issues seriously. This is not a war between men and women. It is a war between women and women-sensitive men against more traditionalist men and women. The war began outside the religious community but has spilled over into it, and we can no longer ignore it, as some quarters of the community at first attempted to do.

It is impossible to write a book like this without making certain sweeping generalizations about men and women. I have often generalized from my own experience as a white, middle-class, middle-aged, long-divorced father. Broad generalizations obviously have many exceptions, so that there will be men and women who do not recognize themselves in some of my claims. But what I have written rings true through my twenty years as an Episcopal priest doing pastoral counseling, and through my much shorter involvement with the men's movement.

NEW ADAM

I have written this book for several reasons. Perhaps the primary one is that I care about the church—about its sexism, its present state of near-bankruptcy, its growing narrowness and judgmentalism, and its increasing inability to offer much of substance to American culture. I am a priest of the church and have committed my life to it. But I am deeply pained by the way an institution that potentially has much to offer now seems to be shunted to the sidelines as irrelevant, largely through its own failure to take the needs of contemporary men and women seriously. Second, I care deeply about men and about women, my fellow beings with whom I share God's creation. It is only within the whole community's working together that there is any hope for the redemption of this world and its rescue from nuclear madness. And third, this book has provided me with an opportunity to work through some of the issues that have been growing inside me for the past few years. Ultimately, therefore, much of this book is highly personal. As Ralph Waldo Emerson observed, "Each truth that a writer acquires is a lantern, which he turns full on what facts and thoughts lay already in his mind, and behold, all the mats and rubbish which had littered his garret become precious."

A repeated source of disagreement throughout the history of the church has been the proper approach to human sexuality. Concepts of resurrection of the soul, an imminent second coming, the taint of inherited sin, and a pervasive spill-over from both Hellenism and Gnosticism all contributed to the church's taking a stance on human sexuality that too often failed to recognize it as a gift from God. Yet at the same time, the fathers of the early church spoke comfortably of the *logos spermatikos* to describe the way in which the creative word of God impregnated creation. The word *Torah* also is built upon an etymological root that means to spurt, impregnate, inseminate, or fertilize. To be spiritually healthy as a Jew or a Christian, men must incorporate into their faith identities their own roles as receptacles, as receivers of God's self-assertion of power, and even the troubling role as a "victim" of God's aggression.

Theology has often spoken of an assumed complementarity of maleness and femaleness; without each other, each is incomplete. The rhetoric of the New Testament and of early church thought is full of such sexually charged images as the church's being the bride of Christ.

4

INTRODUCTION

From feminine imagery to the feminine character of church vestments to the "feminine" qualities that make up sensitive pastoral care, the church has presented an arena in which the retention of a personal masculine identity is full of pitfalls for both the laity and the ordained. Not long ago a student of mine described the struggle to forge a sensitive masculine identity within an institution often described in feminine terms in a paper entitled "I am a Man in a Woman's Body, Screaming to Get Out!" In short, the religious communities of both Judaism and Christianity are self-identified as feminine receivers impregnated by the *logos spermatikos*, the "word-sperm" of God.

In the past two decades, gay liberationists have become increasingly angry at the church's refusal to affirm their sexual identity. But the question to be raised is whether the church has ever affirmed any sexual identity at all. Most heterosexual men within the church are hard-pressed to find ways in which the theological and doctrinal heritage upholds and encourages their sexual orientation and behavior, in spite of the church's having chosen heterosexuality as the norm for human relationships. In this sense, the church's teachings on human sexuality are like the "seed" (pardon the pun!) that fell on rocky soil (Matt. 13:1-9); it took root, sprang up, and quickly withered and died. If the church is to be honest in its dealings with men and women, it must address in a more open manner the variety of human sexual orientations and behaviors. I believe that prayer and human sexuality have a great deal in common. Here I try to address them both, hoping to find a healthier manner in which to integrate them.

When I first sat down to sketch out this book, I kept worrying that the structure of each chapter didn't match the others. Like most American males, I remain entrapped by the principles of logical thinking, parallel structures, and even-handed intellectualism. A recognition of my own imprisonment has helped me worry less about the consistency of the book's structure, and concentrate more on saying some things that I feel deeply. I am also aware that there is little about marriage in this book. It has not been my intention to write about marriage in the 1990s. The institution itself is changing rapidly, with the continuing disintegration of the American nuclear family, and even the church is increasingly unclear about its theology of marriage. A number of books already in print struggle with these issues. Instead I have attempted to concentrate on the way that men relate to their fathers and sons and to each other. My concern is with the friendships and relationships between men.

I also have not attempted to speak much about women, for their experiences are different from men's, and I obviously do not know them first-hand. The women's movement is light-years ahead of the men's movement, and much that has been achieved by feminism has happened because women went away from men to work through their issues. The time has now come for men to go away from women to do our own homework within the intentional community of sensitive men. Until we have sorted through a number of critical same-sex identity issues, we are not ready to build a new future of men and women together. We must build on sameness before we are ready to build on differences.

It is also true that many men already involved in the women's movement have discovered improved relationships with their wives or partners. As men become more sensitive, they also become more aware of what Anthony Astrachan has called "women's struggle for justice and equality." Men become more able to hear women's frustrations, even within their marriages. They become more able to focus on the relationship process instead of on a set of problems to be fixed. Men may learn new ways to value the needs and aspirations of their partners and to make a greater commitment to shared parenting. They may discover new arenas of safety and support as they practice sharing their own emotions with the women who have so long facilitated the assumed masculine tasks of accomplishment and of ordering the universe.

Not everyone will agree with everything I have to say in this book. This is no surprise, for we are all still struggling. The men's movement is young and under fire, and we have not yet created enough opportunities to speak even to each other. When I have presented this material, it has generated anger from men and from women. Yet many men with whom I have spoken yearn to tap into the community of changing men and to discover new opportunities for altered behavior and reconstructed attitudes.

The biggest problem seems to be that most men do not yet understand what hard work this will be for them and for those who love them. Jon Tevlin attended a men's weekend and came away disillusioned:

> By morning I had decided the male wilderness was full of ticks, and that the gods of masculinity were calling elsewhere. I don't know quite what I'd expected from the weekend—perhaps discussion about our goals and fears, about how to get along better with ourselves and with women. Or maybe I just wanted a few laughs with some confident men. But what I found was that insecurity, insincerity, and manipulation still reigned: [lewd] jokes still went unchallenged. . . . If this was indeed a glimpse into the masculinity of the future, then the forest is deeper and darker than I'd imagined.

Cell by cell and individual community by individual community, we men are changing; you, like Tevlin, will know you've gotten there when you lose your tolerance for the typical male attitudes and behavior and start consciously to seek out the company of other men who want things to be different. Again to quote Emerson: "God offers to every mind its choice between truth and repose. Take which you please— you can never have both." I hope this book offers men and men-sensitive women the encouragement to choose truth over repose. At least I believe it is a beginning.

Special thanks are due to a number of persons and organizations who were involved in the development of this book. In particular I am grateful to Joe Ballard, Tom Barnett, Mark Biddle, Mary Boys, Charles Brockett, Susan Crawford, Zev Gotthold, Brit Huckabay for his photography, Hunter and Prestine Huckabay and the organizers of the Thorne-Sparkman School of Religion at St. Paul's, Chattanooga, Tenn., Lee Kiefer, Zilla Kinyon, Joe Marland, and the adult Sunday school class at St. Peter's, Chattanooga, Tenn., Steve Lipscomb, Roy McAlpine, Michael McGarry, Vic McInnis, Davelyn Monti, Mary Margaret Pazdan, Jim Pritchett, John Riggen, Dick Schmidt and the Philadelphia Theological Institute, Arthur Bradford Shippee, Tommy Tipton, Andrew Waldo, Minnie Warburton, Rebecca Abts Wright, Diane Zerfas, OSM, and to my editor at Fortress Press, Michael West.

Biblical texts, particularly as quoted in chapters two through four, are based on the New Revised Standard Version. I have altered or adapted them where I felt that the NRSV translation did not correctly represent the sense of the Hebrew text. Translations of Hebrew texts into English are my own unless otherwise indicated.

PART · ONE

Exercises in Reading Our Own Tradition

CHAPTER · ONE

Explaining Men

Who are men? The question is as old as classical literature and as fresh as the feminist critique. But in our time, as the women in our lives demand equality and justice, as our relationships in the workplace change in bewildering ways, as we struggle to restore the intimacy that we have expected from our relationships with women but lost, and as our assumed positions of privilege crumble, the question has taken on a new urgency for men and for men-sensitive women. Who are men? What drives us? What feeds us emotionally? How can we fill anew the emptiness in our lives? What is the future of our uniquely masculine spirituality? Where can we turn for clarity, for vision, and for a self-understanding that does not embarrass us in the presence of our wives and intimate women friends?

Within the past ten years, we have begun to witness the growth, though nascent, of something called the men's movement, sometimes referred to in academic jargon as "post-feminist men's studies." Post-feminist men's studies is a bit of a misnomer; men cannot themselves be feminist; they can know a lot *about* women, but they can never know how it feels *to be* a woman. Lots of men are not post-feminist, and in many regions, the term "post-feminist" hardly seems to register at all. The field also appears to be threatening to some women, who incorrectly assume that the men's movement represents a trend by

11

men to retrench in the previous despicable traditionalism. I remember the first time I told a feminist friend in a small Southern town that I was giving a speech at a conference on men's studies. She cried in anger and frustration while accusing me of abandoning her in a struggle in which she already had so little support.

As an observer and student of the men's movement, that is not how I understand what is going on. Rather, I see a significant number of men who wish to take the women's movement seriously and have learned much from that movement about human identity in principle, people in general, and men's and women's differences in particular. Men who are attempting to mold the men's movement are not withdrawing their support and encouragement from women's efforts to say who they are and what they need; rather, they are attempting to apply the lessons men learned from the women's movement to men's own sense of identity in a world that has changed quickly. We hope thereby that in a transformed society, men can articulate their identities in support of and in relation to the new ways of living that have rightly developed out of the women's movement.

Some of the observations currently proceeding out of the literature of the men's movement can be organized around four experiences that happen to men so early that men have no control over them. Most men spend the rest of their lives responding to these four experiences: (1) prenatal development from female to male; (2) inability to accommodate determined by anatomy; (3) the learned value of success; and (4) separation/individuation from the mother. Men do not have to be victimized by these early events; instead they can raise their own sensitivities so that they are not entrapped by the dark sides of the male cultural heritage. These four experiences are unique to men— they do not happen in the same way to women. We can understand in these events equal potential for tragedy or creativity.

From Female to Male

The first early experience of men is the biological change from being female into being male. At conception all fetuses are, in nature and in structure, female; it is only six to seven weeks later, when the production of testosterone kicks in due to the presence of the Y chromosome, that some fetuses switch from female to male. Apparently then, it can be said that femaleness is the basic blueprint for animals (and humans), and maleness is simply an overlay. It might also be said that being male is a sort of altered state (some feminists might claim that it is a birth defect), a final state that differs 180 degrees from a man's conceptual beginnings. It can only be concluded that the account of creation in Genesis 2 is backwards: Eve produces Adam, rather than the other way around. Men seem somehow to be male as a kind of afterthought of nature. Such a conclusion is clearly controversial, as is indeed the entire field of psycho-biological determinism, but the work of medical researchers such as Dr. James Michaelson of Harvard and Dr. Estelle Ramey of Georgetown University opens up the possibility that there may be some genetically conditioned drive that inspires men to spend part of their lives trying to overcome that original mutation by trying to convince women that men are the superior of the two sexes.

This kind of postnatal overcompensation takes many forms: the attempts by some men to convince women that they are genitally deficient; the concomitant exaggerated pride that some men take in their own penises or the opposite anxiety that their penises are somehow "too small"; or other men's attempts to convince women that they are dumber or weaker or less capable than men, maybe even less qualified to be ordained, and that these deficiencies are part of the natural order. At least we can say that if there is some sort of psycho-biological predeterminism, it seems not to become dangerous until it is strongly reinforced by the cultural conditioning and sex-role stereotyping that virtually all men and women in our society suffer.

The issue of biological determinism is a dangerous one. As women have correctly pointed out, the argument that biology is destiny—that is, we can only become the product of our individual genetic heritage— creates potential support for theories of genetic superiority and inferiority and ultimately the potential conclusion that women are biologically inferior to men and can thus never really be men's equals. Recognizing these dangers, however, it still must be said that men and women *are* biologically different one from the other. Men have larger brains, but women have larger fibers in the corpus callosum, connecting the right and left hemispheres. Men's brains decrease more in size as they age, and men recover less quickly from strokes that damage the brain. Recent studies by the Kinsey Institute suggest that the male and female brains are different structurally, and probably chemically, and this in turn means that male and female behaviors are going to be different—overlapping but different. Because more hormonal variables are involved in the maturation of the male brain (males are exposed to greater levels of testosterone in their brains) it is possible that boys' higher rates of developmental oddities (left-handedness, nearsightedness, predisposition to allergies, migraines, dyslexia, stuttering, and even abnormal sexual syndromes, all of which are more common in men than in women) may result from the greater potential for error in their neuro-endocrinological development.

Most of our life performance exhibits proof that both culture and education provide opportunities in which we learn to overcome the biogenetic differences between men and women. Yet too much emphasis on social constructionism as the predictable correction to biological determinism also opens up false expectations that individual genetic differences can be eventually overcome by cultural and educational leveling. While the differences between any two men may be much greater than the differences between a given man and woman, it is still true that each of us is a combination of all three factors working on each other: genetic heritage, education and life experience, and cultural particularism. These three factors seem to be able to combine in a remarkable variety of ways, each perceived as a valid expression of masculinity. As David Gilmore observes: "Manliness is a symbolic script, a cultural construct, endlessly variable, and not always necessary." Biology is destiny *and* culture is destiny.

As men grow, they learn, according to Anthony Astrachan, that as men they have four kinds of power: (1) the power to name; (2) the power to mobilize destructive aggression; (3) the power to organize societal, economic, and political life; and (4) the power to direct others' uses of skills. Men learn that all these forms of power can be used to keep women in a position of inferiority, if men so choose and women cooperate. Men learn to use the power of naming against women by controlling language, by teaching women their place in the world through the words which people use to communicate. Men learn to use the power to mobilize destructive aggression against women by abusing them physically, sexually, and emotionally (over 90 per cent of women in the Hite Report [*Women and Love*, 1987] report being emotionally and psychologically harassed by the men they love) and by defining human worth in terms of the ability to be strong enough to go to war. Men learn to use the power to organize societal, economic, and political life against women by excluding them or by refusing to share with them the knowledge necessary to enter these arenas as equals. And men learn to use the power to direct others' use of skills against women by directing women to continue to play secondary roles that will keep men in the limelight and in power. Of course most of these forms of power are traditionally handed to men by society or learned from men such as our own fathers, but men succumb to the temptation to use them, perhaps, because men are still struggling with a competition which originates in the womb.

Nonaccommodation and Loneliness

A second experience that happens long before men have any control over their own destiny is that they are born with anatomical differences that seem to predetermine a course of male loneliness. Anatomically women are born with the capacity to accommodate; they can accommodate vaginally, and they can accommodate in utero (a single form of womanpower against which men have traditionally used all their other forms of power), but anatomically males seem to be able to accommodate no one. This early "accident" appears also to have consequential long-term ramifications. In relationships men seem much slower to accommodate than women. Some men have extraordinary resentments over a woman's ability to nurture inside her a child. Men do not nurture inside, but they do tend to bottle up inside. And men, who are anatomically not accommodating, seem most strongly to express this fact by going through life without friends. Virtually every study done on men and friendships reveals that men rarely have close friendships during their adult lives, except sometimes with their wives, though even that seems to be the exception. Judith Viorst tells of a man who described his relationship with his three best friends: "There are some things I wouldn't tell them. For example, I wouldn't tell them about my work because we have always been highly competitive. I certainly wouldn't tell them about my feelings of any uncertainties with life or various things I do. And I wouldn't talk about any problems I have with my wife or in fact anything about my marriage and sex life. But other than that I would tell them anything." After a brief pause, he laughed and said: "That doesn't leave a hell of a lot, does it?"

Men learn to talk about things that men consider to be safe. Studies of male conversation patterns reveal that men limit their conversations with each other to five safe areas: their professional success; sexual conversation, usually dirty, about women; political issues; sports; and equipment such as guns, sound systems, and computers. Men learn early, even from the cradle, not to talk about feelings or fears or weaknesses with women, and particularly not with men. Studies show that female babies are picked up more often when they cry than male babies. Parents unconsciously try to teach their male babies that a man's crying will produce no results. The research of Lawrence Kohlberg and Carol Gilligan suggests that boys see problems as something to be solved like a math equation, and girls put problems into a larger, more complex, ongoing context. In the same manner, masculine theology sets up differences and oppositions, while feminist theology emphasizes connections. Men learn to be independent and self-sufficient, and men learn to be rugged loners. Writer Herb Goldberg says: "We become anesthetized and robotized because we have been heavily socialized to repress and deny almost the total range of emotional and human needs in order that nothing interfere with our 'masculine' style of goal-directed, task-oriented, self-assertive behavior." Yet of course we cannot suppress our capacity for feelings generally without suppressing our capacity for sexual feeling. To be alive includes being sexually alive, and in suppressing one source of vitality, we suppress another.

It is no wonder, given these beginnings, that Goldberg could also observe: "Asking a man to feel is like taunting a crippled person to run." Men pay a price for being so unaccommodating and so anesthetized. Sometimes they binge or go crazy by hitting women or getting drunk or having a destructive affair; sometimes they get resentful that they are not understood by the women who say they love them; sometimes they develop psychopathological diseases common to the repression of feelings, like bowel problems or headaches or ulcers. Fatal diseases more likely in women between forty-five and sixty-four are asthma and high blood pressure. Fatal diseases more likely in men of the same age are emphysema, atherosclerosis, ischemic heart disease, cerebro-vascular disease, liver disease, other selected heart diseases, and stomach or duodenal ulcers. Sometimes men despair of the loneliness they feel and so force themselves even farther away from relationships; and sometimes they numb the pain of being so self-sufficient through alcohol or drugs or compulsive and consuming work. And they justify all these twisted reactions by saying, "A man's gotta do what a man's gotta do."

The Lesson of Success

A third experience that happens to men very early in their lives is that they learn the value of success. In the poignant lines of her poem "Doing it differently," Marge Piercy writes: "remember that every son had a mother/whose beloved son he was,/and every woman had a mother/whose beloved son she wasn't." A boy learns to earn the gleam in his mother's eye by doing well, and so begins the lifelong male pattern of behavior that says men gain the attention of women by being successful, and so men know who they are by being successful. The workplace becomes the arena where many men express their idea of what masculinity is supposed to look like. Such men express it competitively with other men, but in spite of this competition with other men, they continue to exclude women, because at least men know what the rules of the game are.

Men learn to measure their worth by whether they have fulfilled their vocational or professional hopes and dreams and whether they have been good enough at it that society (we might also say the church) awards them a degree of status. And men carefully guard their work arena from any interference, for it is only in their work arena that they are at all clear about who they are and whether they are worth anything. Men strive for what Daniel Levinson calls "becoming one's own man," which means pursuing a professional dream, setting goals, and then driving to achieve them, all of which take an enormous amount of self-investment and energy. Men learn that they find happiness by performing and that they find women by performing. This performance includes repressing their feelings of being exploited by society.

Men must face that they are compromising themselves; whatever they are doing to succeed and thereby to be reassured that they are masculine, is simultaneously turning them into something that they don't like and don't want to be. Men work hard to repress their feelings of being exploited, because their exploitation deems them weak and powerless. But since men can't be weak and powerless (because then they would be women), they must continue to convince themselves that they are strong and powerful even when they're not. They must become careful not to talk to other men too much about their jobs, so that other men won't find out that these men are powerless. For many men, the lesson of success leads them to commit themselves to work, because that is the only way they know to commit themselves to their families. For most men, working too hard is the primary way they try to be effective parents.

Separation from the Mother

A fourth male experience, which begins around age three, is the anxious process of separating from the most powerful woman in their lives, their mother. Male children develop what Samuel Osherson calls a symbiosis anxiety, that is, a fear of over-identification with women. Not only must men separate from their powerful mothers— they face two additional complications. First, they are surrounded by women: they have women babysitters, most people who work in places where they go with their mothers are women, and almost all primary and elementary school teachers are women. Boys spend the first ten years or so of their lives surrounded by women, and they must work hard to remain separate from them and to avoid over-identification with them.

The second complication arises when boys try to turn away from mother and other women to father or some other man with whom they can identify. For many boys there is no father to turn to. Father is at work, or if he is at home, he is emotionally and/or physically unavailable. The lesson boys learn is that to be masculine means to be rejecting, incompetent, or absent. In most cases this is a tragic misunderstanding of the father's intentions, but it is nonetheless the lesson that most boy children deduce out of their limited experience. As infants and children, we love our fathers, but when they are absent, we must interiorize and then bury our homoerotic longings for them. The most common future outlet is friendship with other men; if we don't form these, we will always mourn the lost homoerotic relationships with our fathers in a twisted way.

As today's fathers realize how much they were hurt, they are attempting to express their affection more openly, although they have not yet determined to restructure their professional lives. In the *New York Times*, 18 February 1990, Anna Quindlen observed, ". . . fathers today do seem more emotional with their children, more nurturing, more open. Many say, 'My father never told me he loved me,' and so they tell their own children they love them all the time. When they're home."

Men learn to fear all things that smack of women or of femininity, and in the absence of a male role model, they learn to walk around alone in pain. But here the lessons are perhaps the strangest lessons of all, for here male sexuality becomes tragically warped. Men learn to desire women sexually, and yet they fear being absorbed by them or over-identifying with them. They yearn for fathers yet learn to keep their distance from physical contact with men, because that is feminine, and men must reject feminine activities for fear of becoming feminine. We err by setting up an artificial opposition between masculinity and femininity. At times it sounds almost as though femininity were something contagious; for example, homosexual elementary school teachers are said to be "contagious," a threat to true masculinity.

Men learn to desire women and yet readily admit that they do not understand them. Even Freud admitted he was "psychologically unable to solve the riddle of femininity." Men learn to desire women and yet fear them. As Warren Farrell writes: "Look at the praying mantis or the black widow spider. The male and female are making sex. The male gets so involved he cannot undo himself. The female satisfies herself, then bites off the head of the male. The male is so locked into the sexual act that he cannot prevent himself from being consumed. The ultimate in vulnerability." This is many men's experience with women. Many married men will admit to an occasional overwhelming fear when coming home at the end of the work day. They are suddenly afraid to enter the house, to hear the sounds of the family in the kitchen, and feel like they are about to be swallowed up. So men stay at work, or they walk in the door with an isolation barrier already surrounding them to protect them from their own families.

Yet at the same time that men fear the women from whom they have struggled so hard to separate themselves, they are sexually drawn to them, even against their wills. Perhaps this desire is something else: perhaps men realize that in a man's world without friends, the one hope men have of friendship is a wife. Or perhaps men want to live out the deeply repressed feminine side of themselves by marrying and allowing their wives to express the husband's own feminine side from a safer distance.

Men do marry, sometimes again and again. Yet they also fear commitment. Commitment for many women means achieving their primary fantasy of a home and a family and security; for many men it means giving up their primary fantasy of success and independence and widely available sex. Sometimes men also realize that they are being used by the women they marry. Men have worked hard to earn their success, whatever it may be, but there are women who will seize the opportunity to have that success in an instant just by marrying it and who will keep it long after the men die young. That is what Warren Farrell calls "women's flashdance to power and status."

Not only do men learn an odd way of relating to women, they also learn an odd way of relating to men. Men yearn to find the father who was never there, and yet they fear intimacy with men, for that intimacy implies that the men themselves are feminine. We teach men in our society a most crippling form of homophobia. If fathers have been physically affectionate with their sons at an early age, they stop holding and kissing their sons somewhere about the age of five, although they continue holding and kissing their daughters until they reach puberty. Men learn that physical touch is sexually loaded, and so men learn to fear touching a man or being touched by one. Often our fear causes us to skip a critical stage in male ego individuation. The skip is potentially disastrous when we have already lost all opportunity for traditional adolescent rites of passage.

Joyce McDougall observes that adolescent homosexuality is a natural extension of our personality, as we create the perfect friend in

20

another person of our same sex. In order to sort out the "you" and the "not you," a young man must pass through a phase when other young men are his love objects for they are the perfectly projected creations of himself. Narcissistic idealization is a defense mechanism by which we develop a sense of self. The idealization is then normally devalued once the individual self is identified and developed. From there, we may deal with our growing fear of homosexuality by constructing an artificially black-and-white world, ignoring the Kinsey scale of human sexual orientation and the fact that most real homosexuality (the term was not coined until a hundred years ago) is constitutional, rather than volitional. As a constitutional condition, even Freud, in a 1935 letter, recognized that "homosexuality is assuredly no advantage, but it is nothing to be ashamed of, no vice, no degradation, it cannot be classified as an illness. . . ."

Men become so fearful of homosexuality that they cut off a large portion of their innate human potential for both growth and intimacy, for by cutting themselves off from other men, they cut themselves off from forty-nine percent of the human race. The women's movement is light-years ahead of the men's movement on this score, for women long ago learned how much other women can give them in terms of healing and supportive physical touch. Men have learned instead the "correct" ways to be physically intimate with another man: hit him, like football players slap each other's bottoms, or hug another man from the chest up, all the while pounding his back (notice the way males pass the peace to each other during worship). Men learn that men do not care for men, so men go through life not caring for other men. Men also go through life not caring for themselves as men or for their bodies, and so they die eight to ten years earlier than women.

Men learn that what men do instead of being intimate is mutilate each other, in war, in the business world, or even on the football line, while women stand on the side and cheer them on. Masculinity exists primarily in the eye of the beholder, but we cultivate a bevy of beholders in order to reassure ourselves. Men get so used to competing with each other that they do not know how to nurture each other. Or they mistake male-bonding and the tenuous loyalty that goes with it for intimacy. Or they get so involved with what Letty Pogrebin calls "men's life-long pissing contest" that they never learn how to tell other men anything that really matters, or even to tell other men the truth. For example, research studies indicate that men who feel strongest about men appearing masculine are the most likely to drop out of therapy. They will not even tell themselves the truth. The ways that men learn to relate to women in our American society are tragic. But the ways men learn to relate to other men are equally tragic.

Sociologist Don Sabo writes of his own high school athletic career:

> Today, I no longer perceive myself as an individual ripped off by athletic injury. Rather I see myself as just one more man among many men who got swallowed up by a social system predicated on male domination. Patriarchy has two structural aspects. First it is a hierarchical system in which men dominate women in crude and debased, slick and subtle ways. . . . But it is also a system of intermale dominance, in which a minority of men dominates the masses of men. . . . Patriarchy's mythos of heroism and its morality of power-worship implant visions of ecstasy and masculine excellence in the minds of the boys who ultimately will defend its inequities and ridicule its victims. . . . Male competition for prestige and status in sport and elsewhere leads to identification with the relatively few males who control resources and are able to bestow rewards and inflict punishment.

It is men themselves who made "non-male" behavior by males a punishable crime.

From these four lessons, men have been handed a heritage that attempts to define what it means to be masculine. From the first early occurrence, beginning female and turning into male, men learn to define themselves as the ones with the penises, even to the point of developing the opposite of penis envy, that is, penis pride. (On another level, of course, it can be claimed that the erect penis does not belong exclusively to men, for it is the symbol around which both men and women often organize their sexual fantasies.) From the early lesson of being built not to accommodate, men learn to define themselves as strong, independent, and self-sufficient, regardless of the cost. From the early lesson of being a beloved son, men learn to define themselves on the basis of success and achievement. And from the early lesson of turning away from mother, men learn to define themselves on the basis of a controlled sexual prowess with women and a phobic distancing from men. The four marks, then, of the traditional American male are: penis pride, rugged self-sacrificing independence, professional success and status, and a mixture of sexual activity with women and a frequently pathological homophobia.

Developing a New Masculine Agenda

This would seem to be an accurate description of what might be called the male condition. I don't think, however, that the male condition is all bad; in fact, I know a lot of happy men, myself included. But even the happy men that I know would like things to be different, not because women tell us that things need to be different, but because deep down inside our human selves, men know that we need not be imprisoned for our whole lives by these four early experiences.

I also know a lot of men who right now are responding to the women's movement with a mixture of rage and confusion. Although I can also empathize with the bitter frustration of women who time after time have men turn away from listening to them, it seems that confrontive criticism often heard from the women's movement is about the worst way to effect change in anyone. The criticism at times comes from unexpected quarters. Freeman Dyson tells the following humorous story, with a bitter edge:

> I cannot regard humanity as a final goal of God's creation. Humanity looks to me like a magnificent beginning but not the last word. Small children often have a better grasp of these questions than grown-ups. It happened to me that I adopted a stepdaughter. I moved into her family when she was five years old. Before that, she had been living alone with her mother. Soon after I moved in, she saw me for the first time naked. "Did God really make you like that?" she asked with some astonishment. "Couldn't he have made you better?"

Instead of expending their energies being angry or confused by the women's movement, a better approach would be for men to get their own acts together and to set for themselves a threefold agenda: (1) supporting those requests from the women's movement that they know will enhance the rich heterogeneity of humankind and affirm women as having been created in God's image; (2) plotting concrete ways to change how men's traditional sex-stereotyping heritage imprisons

23

them; and (3) affirming the many experiences and characteristics of being male that are good and creative and constructive.

I like much about being male. I like work, even the extremely stressful parts. I, like virtually every human being, like power, although I try to be cautious about its misuse. I like my body the way it is, and I like taking care of it through regular exercise and diet. But there are some things I would change, three in particular: (1) I wish men were better about feeling and expressing those feelings. I believe we can learn this, not through criticism but through coaxing and encouragement by women who still have the patience to help. (2) I wish men would radically change the way they parent so that when little boys and little girls individuate from their mothers, there really is a father to turn to. (3) I wish men would learn new ways to relate to other men physically, through tenderness instead of pounding on each other, and most importantly, through emotional intimacy, divorced from crippling homophobia. I think we can learn to feel, parent, and relate to other men differently, and I think that the best way to learn is through men helping other men, perhaps in support groups similar to those modeled for us by the women's movement. Katharine Hepburn is reported to have said: "Sometimes I wonder if men and women really suit each other. Perhaps they should live next door and just visit now and then." As we sort out who we are, there may be more truth to this than humor.

But even support groups seem hard for us. Letty Pogrebin tells the story of a group of divorced and divorcing men who got together to form a men's support group. In a typically masculine way they met, set measurable tasks and goals, accomplished the tasks and goals, and then seeing no further reason to be together, disbanded. We won't have men's support groups as long as we approach them from a business model. But whether through support groups or some other way, men can begin to change most effectively by opening up with other men, by sharing in trust and without competition their hopes and dreams and feelings, their failures and weaknesses and fears. We can start with men rather than with women, for men understand men in the same way that women understand women; the levels of potential trust are already there and don't have to be built from scratch.

EXPLAINING MEN

Too many women either do not understand what we are trying to do or reject it. Todd Erkel uses a memorable image: "The new man, if he has arrived, is being received like an errant package from UPS. Women want to know: Is *this* what they ordered?" If we rely too heavily on women's permission or approval, the package may be refused, returned, without ever being opened to see what is actually inside.

In spite of what the most radical branches of the women's movement are saying, I continue to believe that it is a very good thing to be male. Having said that, I would like to learn how to be male in such a way that my son Jacob and my daughter Katie can grow into a world that is more honest, more peaceful, more sensitive, and more open to the fullest development of both men's and women's potential. That sounds to me like the liberating good news of the gospel of God's generous love. To begin to illustrate the slavery from which men need to be liberated, chapters 3–6 that follow explore some of the Bible stories about men who relate to each other in traditional ways, how these traditional ways produce predictably negative results, and whether the teachings of Jesus provide any new insight into male-male or male-female patterns of relationship. The stories are offered as exercises, but even approached in a theoretical manner they threaten us with feelings of terror.

CHAPTER · TWO

The New Adam Tradition

Change is often frightening for men of any age, for it means the relinquishment of security and of comfortable assumptions. Teens and young men are often hanging on for dear life in a highly competitive world, and new rules and expectations become the enemy as their presumed field of security seems to be shifting. Men of early middle age are usually wrapped up in the identity they draw from their profession, and any change in their conduct or status in the profession threatens to undo their shaky, externally dependent identity. Generally, men of late middle age have finally figured out what to like about themselves and want nothing to change, so that they do not have to ask themselves hard new questions. Only men of senior years have the freedom to relax enough not to be afraid of a fluctuating identity; yet financial and familial security remains a high priority even for our elders who no longer need to prove aggressively their masculine self-perception.

We are particularly susceptible to fearing change when we do not understand where it will take us. In our decade, women are demanding that men change, and we do not know how to respond because we tend to think that change would jeopardize the foundations of our security. Light is what we know, no matter how dim. Darkness is what we do not know: the terrors within, the price we will have to pay to be different, and what is on the other side. We are afraid that if we change, we will have to reject every comfortability of self that we have so painstakingly constructed. British anthropologist Sir Edmund Leach claimed in the 1960s that such binary oppositions—either/or categories—are intrinsic to human thought. Yet in his book *Eclipse of God*, theologian Martin Buber points out the flaw in our human tendency to think in either/or categories: "Each age is, of course, a continuation of the preceding one, but a continuation can be confirmation and it can be refutation." Little in life falls neatly into an either/or category.

We do in fact have an element of choice left to us—what specific elements of our male identity we will seek to confirm, as opposed to what we will refute. We need not "throw out the baby with the bath water." The first step in any change of personal identity is the recognition that change is necessary or good, followed by a critical self-examination, in which we can differentiate what is generally good about who we are from what needs to be systematically deconstructed, redirected, or discarded. The categories of maleness and masculinity are not inherently bad or evil, but neither are they ever free from either the victimizing or the victimization that are the result of our inherited sex-stereotypes, cultural assumptions, and the confusion that is endemic to our personal identities.

Any spectrum that includes the possibilities of confrontation, affirmation, and refutation implies that some things must change, and at times change radically. Classic psychotherapeutic theory has quarrelled over how much, if at all, any person is capable of changing. By 1937, Sigmund Freud had his doubts about whether a change in character was truly possible for human beings. In his essay "Analysis Terminable and Interminable," Freud sought to make clear what limits are set to the efficacy of analytic therapy. Not all problems can be resolved in psychotherapy, he said; only problems that are currently causing frustration to the patient, and can therefore be the cause of transference to the therapist, can be resolved. Since it is inadvisable to attempt to stir up latent problems so that they might be resolved, the prophylactic effect of psychoanalysis is minimal. Freud even expressed doubts about the prospects of preventing a return of any neurosis that had already been treated.

Erich Fromm, however, expressed no misgivings about the possibility of a general and permanent change in a patient's character. Fromm's optimism was made possible by his view of human nature, which was markedly different from Freud's. For Fromm, human nature is essentially good. The "normal" individual possesses within himself or herself the inherent tendency to develop, to grow, and to be productive, and the paralysis of this tendency is in itself the symptom of mental sickness. In *Man for Himself*, Fromm wrote: "Humans are not necessarily evil but become evil only if the proper conditions for their growth and development are lacking. The evil has no independent existence of its own; it is the absence of the good, the result of the failure to realize life."

Both Freud and Fromm, to a greater or lesser degree, were influenced by the Jewish and Christian religious traditions and their definitions of the character of human nature. In the process, both theorists addressed the question of whether a new character could emerge from one's old, or former, character. "Old" and "new" are accepted oppositional categories in both religious traditions, yet psychotherapeutic theory argues that we must scrutinize all such oppositional categories carefully for simplistic assumptions or childish logic. Psychologist Alfred Adler warned that oppositional thinking is frequently the product of an arrested development, for such categories suggest the failure to achieve a mature and sophisticated grasp of reality. The categories "old" and "new" need not necessarily imply the value judgment that old equals bad and new equals good, nor are the two categories necessarily or automatically discontinuous.

Renewal in the Bible and Theology

The old Adam of Genesis 1–2, the first Adam created by God, is of course new, for he is Adam without precedent. He was new, and everything that he observed and experienced was new. But he was as well a new concept, for Adam and his equal and helpmate Havah (the root meaning of the Hebrew name is "life") were the first of creation specifically formed in the image of God. Adam, and the image he contained, remained new for his entire life, indelibly new and indelibly good.

But with that newness and goodness, which each descendant of Adam and Eve inherited, came also an awareness of human failure and a longing for the redemption of creation, which led in turn to conversation of renewal—the "new" made new again. The basic concept of renewal was woven by God into the fabric of creation, in the passage of sun to moon to sun, in the ebb and flow of the seas, in the animal cycle of birth and death, and in the rise and fall of the agricultural seasons. The renewal linked to cycles of nature deeply affected the Semitic peoples, who were tied to the land for survival. Well before the Genesis account was committed to writing, our Semitic ancestors recorded the dramatic struggle of water with drought, the verdant season with the arid season, and the promise of life with the threat of death in the anthropomorphic stories of Marduk and of the battles of Baal with Prince Yamm and Judge Nahar during the month of Tammuz. The Hebrew pilgrim festivals of Sukkot, Passover, and Shavuot had their origins in the cycle of agricultural dependency and were only later sanctified by a carefully articulated theological overlay of monotheistic justification.

An acute awareness of the natural cycles of renewal informs the way that Jer. 31:31-34 should be read:

> Days are surely coming, says the Lord, when I will make a new covenant with the house of Israel, and with the house of Judah. It will not be like the covenant that I made with their ancestors when I took them by the hand to bring them out of the land of Egypt—a covenant that they broke, though I was their husband, says the Lord. But this is the covenant that I will make with the house of Israel after those days, says the Lord: I will put my Torah within them, and I will write it on their hearts; and I will be their God, and they shall be my people. No longer shall they teach one another, or say to each other, "Know the Lord," for they shall all know me, from the least of them to the greatest, says the Lord; for I will forgive their iniquity, and I will remember their sin no more.

Similarly, Isa. 34:4:

> All the host of heaven shall rot away, and the skies roll up like a scroll. All their host shall wither like a leaf withering on a vine, or fruit withering on a fig tree.

29

EXERCISES IN READING OUR OWN TRADITION

Although the Jeremiah passage speaks of the temporal order, and the Isaiah passage of the eschatological order, the foundation metaphor in both passages is the heavens pictured as being rolled as is a Torah scroll—a book familiar by heart that is suddenly made new again, so that new things can be seen and new promises kept. According to the commentary of Amos Chakham to Isa. 34:4: "As the stars fall out of the heavens, so will the letters drop from the Torah scroll at the destruction. The scroll will be erased and rolled up, never to be read again." In either passage, there is no mention of some unprecedented newness, but rather the making new again of that which is already known. The passages speak of the same moon, stars, and heaven as humanity already sees in the night skies. All remain the known same, yet each is also revealed as having been made new again. Only when the stars are no longer renewed, but instead are destroyed altogether, is hope to be lost. The Torah of God is not a new scroll, but the same one that rolls and unrolls, and each time that it is renewed we see it to be something familiar and something new. The image of the Torah scroll thus functions as a metaphor for the inseparability of both continuity and renewal. What allows humanity to continue to live is the constant renovation of the known, rather than the innovation of the unknown.

Until recently, a book meant something bound between two covers, containing cut pages that had to be turned in order to continue a sentence or a thought. A Torah scroll is a long carpet of parchment with columns, which is rolled on wooden rollers, rather than turned like cut pages. These passages from Jeremiah and Isaiah make more sense in our generation, when we have reverted to that ancestral form of written record through the use of word processing, which rolls material up and down a screen. In that sense we gain a renewed understanding of Jer. 31:31-34 and Isa. 34:4. We have as well a better sense of the ancient Jewish festival of Simchat Torah (the Joy of the Torah), on which festal day the last words of Deuteronomy are completed, and the scroll is rolled immediately back to the beginning so that Genesis commences anew on the same day—a continuous revelation symbolized by the rolling and unrolling of the scroll and its text.

Christian theology proceeded quickly to an understanding of the resurrected Christ as the new Adam, through which the old Adam—interpreted metaphorically as all humanity—is redeemed. The poignant legend that the skull of Adam tumbled out from the earth at the foot of the Cross is an effort to picture the renewal of humanity effected by the death of Christ. In this standard Christian parable of the triumph of life over death, old takes on a negative value, in spite of this oppositional paradigm's being inconsistent with the teachings of Jesus. More typical to the teachings of Jesus is an affirmation of the superior value of the old, of the authority of the received tradition, of our inheritance from our forebears. For example, at Luke 5:39, in a parable frequently misunderstood by Christian preachers, Jesus confirms that old wine is preferable to new wine (as any respectable oenophile already knows!). At Matt. 13:51-52, Jesus teaches that those who are in touch with the kingdom understand the correct balance between old and new, realizing that neither is dispensable. In the same vein is the teaching of Jesus at Matt. 12:3-8, in which he is sensitive to the authority of tradition (the old) and yet offers a sense of identity that feels so renewed as to be new.

In the context of history, it is difficult to trace the original intent of these old/new paradigms attributed to Jesus, for this absolute is not strongly typical either of Hellenistic literature or of Hebrew literature, both of which more often value highly the venerable character of antiquity. In the Hellenistic tradition, for example, Heraclitus spoke with deep admiration of the repeated triumph of the old; the continuity of tradition was deeply revered in the Mishnaic tradition, and much innovation was suspect. In fact Christianity has been inconsistent in its use of the new/old paradigm. The category "new" has been used to contrast with "old" Judaism or the old Adam, and yet the "old" is quickly employed to defend tradition, particularly the interpretive tradition of Scripture or liturgical practice.

Renewal as Rabbinic Value

Meanwhile, rabbinic tradition created something different out of the new/old paradigm. Often citing the authority of Jeremiah 31 and Isaiah 34, creative renewal became an important operational rabbinic value.

According to the Mishnaic tractate entitled The Chapters of the Fathers, *Avot 1.13*, Hillel used to say: "Anyone who does not increase shall cease." This is traditionally interpreted to mean that each generation is required to review and repeat its inherited tradition and then to innovate carefully within and upon that tradition, for only through such creative renewal is the tradition kept alive. The later commentator Meiri understood this same quotation as meaning "One who is not always striving to innovate will come to an end, that is to say, the very memory of him will perish. . . ."

The rabbinic commentary entitled Pirkei de Rabbi Eliezer, in chapter 51 on the moon and its phases, develops further the imaginative symbol of the rolling scroll:

> The sages say: "The heavens and the earth are destined to pass away and to be renewed. What is written concerning them? *And the heavens shall be rolled together as a scroll* [Isa. 34:4]." Just as when a person reads in a scroll of the Torah and he rolls it, and again he opens it to read therein and he rolls it (together), likewise in the future will the Holy One, blessed be He, roll together the heavens like a scroll. . . . *And the earth shall wax old like a garment* [Isa. 51:6]; just as a person spreads out his prayer shawl and folds it up, and again he unfolds it and puts it on and renews it (thereby), likewise the Holy One, blessed be He, in the future will fold up the earth and again will He spread it out and put it in its place like a garment. . . . Rabbi Eliezer said: "All the host of heaven in the future will pass away, and will be renewed. What is written concerning them? *And all the host of heaven shall be dissolved* [Isa. 34:4]." Just as the leaves fade from off the vine and the fig tree, and the stocks remain standing as a dry tree, and again they blossom afresh and bear buds and produce new leaves and fresh leaves; likewise in the future will all the host of heaven fade away, and they will return and will again be renewed in order to make known before Him that there is passing away (which) does not (really) pass away. No more shall there be hunger nor evil, neither plague nor misfortunes, as it is said, *For behold I create new heavens and a new earth* [Isa. 65:17]. Rabbi Jannai said: "All the hosts of heaven pass away and are renewed every day. What are the hosts of heaven? The sun, the moon, the stars, and the constellations. Know that it is so. Come and see, that when the sun sets in the west, it bathes in the waters of the Ocean; it is like a man who extinguishes his lamp by dipping it in the water.

Such are the waters of the Ocean, for with the setting of the sun it seems to disappear, and it has no flame all night long until it comes to the east. When it arrives at the east it washes itself in the river of fire, like a man who kindles his lamp in the midst of the fire. Likewise the sun kindles its lamps and puts on its flames and ascends to give light upon the earth, and it renews every day the work of the Creation."

Continuity is an integral part, but not the sole component, of renewal. Echoing the Socratic method, the early medieval rabbinic commentator Rashi argued in his interpretation of Deut. 11:13 that one cannot grasp anything new unless it relates to something one has known all along, so that the new grows out of the old without destroying it. The insight of any inquirer both confirms prior knowledge and experience and adds to it, so that the old is suddenly new. Danish theologian Soren Kierkegaard observed that what we knew yesterday seems childish or even foolish in light of what we know today. Each new lesson brings new clarity to the tradition of the past and to the possibilities of the present.

At times, this process of renewing identity is called "rebirth" in the rabbinic tradition (see for example Kehati's *Mishnayot*, Nezikin Baba Metzia 2:11). Rebirth is the re-education that brings one to a higher level of clarity and a restructuring of one's scale of values. Such re-education and clarity is a form of both intellectual and spiritual birth, paralleling or even surpassing in importance one's physical birth. Such developmental values are foundational to Western civilization; hence the elevated role of a teacher or mentor in the rabbinic, Hellenistic, and early Christian traditions.

Yet with all this, there is no doubt that change, even with its affirming character of rebirth, is jarring. This story is told of a fourth-century Christian monk:

Athanasius of holy memory asked Abba Pambo to come down from the desert to Alexandria. When he arrived, he saw a woman that was an actress, and wept. And the bystanders asked him why he wept. And he said, "Two things grieved me. The first was her damnation; the second, that I take less trouble about pleasing God than she takes about pleasing the dregs of society."

EXERCISES IN READING OUR OWN TRADITION

A giant of Hebrew literature, Shemuel Yosef Agnon, in his book *Days of Awe*, recounts the story of a great teacher who was shocked by the need to change his own personal character:

> I have heard it said of Rav Saadiya Gaon that once one of his students arrived unexpectedly in the middle of the night and found him wallowing in the snow. The student stood there astounded, frightened, and trembling. He cried out, "O Master! Master! You certainly need no affliction nor severe mortification such as this in order to restore your righteousness! If so honorable a person as you, who never soiled himself with sin, or even with sinful thoughts, mortifies his flesh in this way, what is left for us who are mere weedy moss on the wall, who have been engaged in sinning as long as we can remember, and yet have no means of self-mortification which would ever balance our score?"
>
> R. Saadiya Gaon answered him, "Indeed! I am not aware of having offended my Maker by any such sin of commission or omission. It is not my conduct which requires atonement. I am bothered by my *attitude* which stands in need of correction—a lesson that I learned from a simple innkeeper. I shall relate the incident to you.
>
> "On one of my journeys, I sought lodging in a wayside inn. As I was dressed simply, without the habit befitting my station, the innkeeper had no way of telling who was this guest asking for his hospitality. Hence he received me politely, as he would any wayfaring Jew. Someone at the inn must have recognized me and spread the word throughout the town, that I was staying at the inn. Soon the townsfolk came to call upon me to pay homage and obeisance. I noticed that the innkeeper seemed at a loss to understand the commotion. However, he was guided by the attitude of my callers, and began to serve drinks and delicacies in order to make them a festive reception. After hours of Torah talk, I wished to retire to my quarters, and so bid them farewell with a blessing. After they had left, the innkeeper ran over to me, fell on his knees, and started sobbing uncontrollably with bitter tears. In a racked voice, he begged my pardon, humbling himself and imploring me that no slight was intended when he received me as he would any ordinary wayfarer. Of course I appeased him, and told him that he was not guilty of any slight or insult because he acted out of ignorance. (Now that we have become better acquainted, I am certain that he will always receive me as my dignity merits.)
>
> "I then repaired to my quarters, and like him, fell on my knees. I wept and prayed to my God to grant me His pardon. With growing

cognizance from day to day, I realized that the manner in which I served Him yesterday was not befitting my understanding of Him today. I then resolved that on account of this impropriety, I shall have to do penance as long as I live."

From Insight to Change

Within the process of cultivating a renewed spiritual identity, one must address that form of repentance (*teshuvah*) that is prompted by intellectual growth and conceptual breakthrough, rather than by sin and guilt. One must be on the alert, while progressing in relating to one's environment and while gaining new insights through the creative process of an active mind, that one continues to move constantly from infantilism to a more mature wisdom. I catch myself in shock: How could my notions and conclusions of yesterday have been satisfactory when I come today to revise my whole outlook on my human and physical environment and my relationship to God?

Both Socrates and Kierkegaard cherished such moments of revelation and understood this lightning illumination as the truest form of conversion. Through conversion and renewal of my identity, I reach a higher level of understanding. Not all the problems of yesterday are solved, but they appear suddenly insignificant from the new vantage point I have gained. In the New Testament, we find such a higher level of awareness illustrated at John 20:28. There, "doubting" Thomas is moved by lighting illumination; he recognizes Jesus' divine character and demands to touch the wounded hands of the postresurrection Christ. Thomas exclaims: "My master and my God." His teacher, in a moment of clarity, is revealed as the incarnation of the Holy One.

Sexism, assumptions of superiority, culturally inherited sex stereotyping, antithetical thinking, emotional sterility, the unexamined perpetuation of tradition—all are forms of a frozen attitude in urgent need of conversion and renewal. Such conversion and renewal are possible only if one remains vigilant and alert to one's own constant potential for growth and change. This sensitivity to identity transformation is no reason to belittle as infantile what one has achieved yesterday. Just as it would be ridiculous for an adult man to be ashamed that he was ever a baby, so we need not be ashamed of a previous identity, even a sexist one, as long as we are already in the process of conversion and renewal.

In the early rabbinic period, the question arose whether such renewal changes our habits or our personality or essence. According to the Pesikta deRav Kahana (Mandelbaum, I.120):

> This is the fire offering which you shall offer to the Lord: two lambs (*kvsym*) a year old without blemish day by day for a continual burnt offering [Num. 28:3]. The school of Shammai [disagrees with] the school of Hillel [over the correct reading of *kvsym*]. The school of Shammai says "lamb" should be read as referring to the subjugation (*kvs*) of the sins of Israel, as it is said "He will again have compassion on us; he will tread down our iniquities" [Micah 7:19]. The school of Hillel says "lamb" should be read as referring to the sacrifices which launder (*kvs*) away the sins of Israel, as it is written "Though your sins be like scarlet, they shall be white as snow" (Isa. 1:18).

For the school of Shammai, habits can be suppressed but not changed, while for the school of Hillel, character itself is changed through purification. Such an interpretation is supported by even earlier manuscripts of the Pesikta in which the school of Hillel retorts to the school of Shammai: "Anything that is simply suppressed will rise to the surface again."

We may resolve this tension between the schools of Hillel and Shammai, and of Freud and Fromm, by realizing that we change our habits first, which should in turn alter our personal values, but without altering our essence. As an old axiom so correctly observes, "Attitude changes follow behavior changes." For example, I may have the personal habit of dropping sexist remarks. Stopping such remarks will soon lead to a change in the way I value women. Such a second step signals a change in my personal values, though my essence as a male and child of God remains the same. As my behavior and values change, I am free to recognize what is true and good about my essence as a male. The old Adam is affirmed by the emergence of the new Adam, but the old will remain denied until such time that the new Adam emerges. The new teaches the true lasting value of the old, transformed.

Recently, in his important essay, "Lonely Man of Faith," Rabbi Joseph Soloveitchik addressed the paradigm of old Adam/new Adam, although he uses the terms "first Adam" and "second Adam." First Adam (drawing on Genesis 1) is Adam the master of technology, and second Adam (drawing on Genesis 2) is Adam the partner in community. By analogy, Soloveitchik's systematization contrasts an unexamined, unredeemed traditional masculinity and the new masculinity emerging as a result of the challenge of feminism, though of course it is not this contemporary issue to which he refers. Soloveitchik writes,

> The two Adams do not concur in their interpretations of the objective they pursue. The idea of humanity, the great challenge summoning man to action and movement, is placed by them in two incommensurate perspectives. While Adam the first wants to reclaim himself from a closed-in, non-reflective, natural existence by setting himself up as a dignified majestic being capable of ruling his environment, Adam the second sees his separateness from nature and his existential uniqueness not in dignity or majesty but in something else. There is, in his opinion, another mode of existence through which man can find his own self, namely, the redemptive, which is not necessarily identical with the dignified. Quite often, an existence might be replete with dignity and mastery, and yet remain unredeemed.

Adam the first and Adam the second relate very differently to wives and lovers. Each is lonely, but Adam the first uses women for his own ends, including the achievement of his self-oriented tasks and goals, while Adam the second engages his helpmate as part of the voluntary sacrificial community that will effect the redemption of creation. Soloveitchik differentiates the two:

> According to the Biblical story, God was not concerned with the loneliness of Adam the first. Neither was Adam aware of the pronouncement . . . "It is not good for man to be lonely." . . . Adam the first, representing the natural community, would translate this pronouncement into pragmatic categories, referring not to existence as such, but to productive work. If pressed for an interpretation of the pronouncement, he would paraphrase it: It is not good for man to work alone. . . . The words *I shall make him a helpmate* would refer, in accordance with his social philosophy, to a functional partner to whom it would be assigned to collaborate with and assist Adam the first in his undertakings, schemes, and projects. . . . Adam the second is still lonely.

He is a citizen of a new world, the world of man, but he has no companion with whom to communicate and therefore he is existentially insecure. . . . At this crucial point, if Adam is to bring his quest for redemption to full realization, he must initiate action leading to the discovery of a companion who, even though as unique and singular as he, will master the art of communicating and, with him, form a community. However, this action, since it is part of the redemptive gesture, must also be sacrificial. . . . This new companionship is not attained through conquest, but through surrender and retreat. *And the eternal God caused an overpowering sleep to fall upon the man.* Adam was overpowered and defeated—and in defeat he found his companion. . . . The community-fashioning gesture of Adam the first is . . . purely utilitarian and intrinsically egotistic and, as such, rules out sacrificial action. For Adam the second, communicating and communing are redemptive sacrificial gestures.

Few words could capture more perfectly the tragic manner in which American males are victimized by our cultural inheritance of rugged individualism, to the exclusion of the possibilities open to us in the human community intended by God for our conversion and renewal, and the redemption of creation.

The tension Soloveitchik identifies in the opening chapters of Genesis stems from the fact that the two Adams are not two separate people, but one. God did not create two Adams, but one: he both desires power and success and is lonely and reaches out in genuine desire for the community. Adam the one, both first and second, is Adam of internal self-confrontation, Adam in tension, Adam who is at the same time "I" and "Thou," Adam whom we see recreated in contemporary sensitive men in transition. Ultimately Adam the second must confront Adam the first within each of us, in order to say, "You must make room for me, in order that either of us may live." Though he assumes that Adam the first comes naturally, and Adam the second must be cultivated, Soloveitchik points out,

Rejection of either aspect of humanity would be tantamount to an act of disapproval of the divine scheme of creation which was approved by God as being very good. As a matter of fact, men of faith have accepted Adam the first a long time ago. Notwithstanding the fact that Adam the second is the bearer of a unique commitment, he remains also a man of majesty who is inspired by the joyous spirit of creativity and constructive adventure.

New Adam Emerges

Ultimately the second Adam emerges only in community, and since community depends upon commitment, I would argue that it emerges most healthily within the community of sensitive men. Martin Buber wrote of committed encounter in his book *I and Thou*. A careful examination of Buber's work reveals that he is not inhibited by the trite paradigm of male/female complementarity; rather, the "Thou" by which any "I" becomes fully "I" can be *any* other person who brings us to wholeness. In fact, as Buber admits in his book *Between Man and Man*, the encounter that brought him to the realization of his fundamental principle of relationship was a chance encounter with "a broad dapple-gray horse." He goes on to observe that the fullness of our sexual identity, our masculinity, is not dependent upon meeting our opposite sex, but upon meeting any "other" who prompts in us a desire for unity, absorption, and union—eros rather than agape. The new Adam emerges in community between vulnerable human beings in transition and in turn is the fullest expression of the proper relationship between humanity and God (the true I-Thou encounter).

The courageous new Adam—the reborn and humanized technological Adam—emerges through singing, through storytelling, and through silence.

Through singing: In *The Prophet*, Lebanese poet Khalil Gibran presents the image of marriage as two pillars of a temple, standing side by side; each is to maintain a separate identity, while working in complete harmony to support the structure of society. The question that remains for many is how much one can share, as for example in marriage, and yet not lose one's sense of personal privacy in identity. The work of Murray Bowen and Edwin Friedman makes clear that secrets render family systems dysfunctional. But does the fear of secrets mean that everything must be told and shared in a committed relationship? Where is the line beyond which sharing or giving up means losing one's identity? Where is the point of privacy-of-soul that not only cannot be shared, but is even inappropriate to share?

EXERCISES IN READING OUR OWN TRADITION

In the early days of Jewish immigration, two theories competed. Israel Zangwill argued in favor of the melting pot, in which individual identities were subsumed in a homogeneity, whereas Louis Brandeis advocated that society should be like an orchestra, in which each instrument is trained to play with its own individual integrity to create a harmonious whole, but without losing its unique identity. Yet even Brandeis' theory omits a crucial element of personal identity: the song we each sing is intended for no ears but our own. Singing in the privacy of the shower is as critical a part of identity as playing harmoniously in the orchestra. I am listening to my singing: that is my soul, and it is not intended to become public information. It is my most private self, and whatever of it I share publicly, even if only with a committed partner, is lost to me forever.

If there is one memory of my relationship with my father that I regret deeply, it is of interfering with the beauty of his private singing. As a musical child, I had a trained ear at an early age. My father sang lustily in the shower, though not at all well. One day, with a child's frankness, I asked my mother in a voice intended for my father to overhear, "Mom, why do men sing so awful?" From that day, I never heard my father sing again. Only now do I realize that my complaint destroyed a beautiful component of his private identity—his unique instrument, whose music was first intended for his ears alone, though indispensable to the orchestral consonance of humanity.

Through storytelling: Each of us has a unique story to tell, particular to our individual experiences and perceptions. Memory and retelling keep those stories alive; conversion and renewal allow us to reshape those stories and thus make ourselves new again, even though the facts of the past can never be erased. Each time we tell our particular stories, we enter again into those experiences, including their context and emotions. At times we also make other people's stories our own stories, and at other times our individual stories become stories that embody the memory of a whole community. Of concern in this story development is the distinction between the German concepts of *Historie* (factual history) and *Geschichte* (story history), or of *erklären* (explanation) and *verstehen* (understanding), or in English, the distinction between meaning and significance. In the assimilation of our own stories with those of the intentional community of men, objective history becomes a personal memory. We cherish the stories, telling and retelling them, but at the same time guarding "the text." Just as new Adam is built on the continuation and affirmation of the old, so new hearings of the meaning of a story are built on the continuity of the received text. Only by telling the same story again can we hear something new in it each time. If we change the story, or worse, if we forget the story, nothing new will be heard. By changing the story, we not only destroy the past, but we also destroy our own future. We have a spiritual identity only insofar as we re-enact and then reshape in our individual lives the same redemptive stories of our corporate communities.

Through silence: The Jewish philosopher and theologian Andre Neher has written movingly of the silence of God. Musicians know that the shape of a melody is determined as much by the silences, or rests, written into it as by the notes that comprise its overt form. Silence is an important and private commodity, and like stories, it can also become an integral part of the dynamic of a committed community. To walk with a friend for miles without talking is a sign of intense trust and of patience and caring developed over a long time. One of the great joys of the men's group in which I participate is those times when we sit in silence for long minutes, with no one talking. This is perhaps the deepest form of friendship, to be in the communion and intimate security of knowing yourself in the company of a kindred soul.

In this combination of singing, storytelling, and silence, Christians and Jews alike will recognize the community of worship. In singing, in storytelling, in silence, Christians meet in community the Christ, who as new Adam holds out the opportunity for rebirth. As our mentor, Christ offers us the opportunity for the recovery of life, the higher levels of clarity and the restructuring of our priorities, the courage and trust to recognize the other as Thou within the community of men who seek renewal and rebirth. As participants of the new creation, we find fresh opportunities to explore the broad range of spiritual disciplines, a gentler but more secure sense of self within relationship and societal systems, and a renewed commitment to connectedness with both earth and nature, unrolling and rerolling like an endless Torah scroll, ever familiar, ever new.

CHAPTER • THREE

The Child Is the
Father of the Man
*King David and
His Son Absalom*

Several years ago, Phyllis Trible, professor of Hebrew Bible at the Union Theological Seminary, published her extraordinary book, *Texts of Terror: Literary-Feminist Readings of Biblical Narratives*, in which she meditates on the biblical accounts of the lives of four women who are victims of their society's assumptions: Hagar (Genesis 16 and 21), Tamar (2 Samuel 13), the unnamed concubine from Bethlehem (Judges 19), and the daughter of Jephthah (Judges 11). She calls these four stories texts of terror because, like Jacob at the River Jabbok, these women, victimized by the male heroes of the Scriptures, wrestled demons in the night, without a compassionate God to save them. She writes of women who hear these texts:

> In combat we wonder about the names of the demons. Our own names, however, we all too frightfully recognize. The fight itself is solitary and intense. We struggle mightily, only to be wounded. But yet we hold on, seeking a blessing: the healing of wounds and the restoration of health. If the blessing comes—and we dare not claim assurance—it does not come on our terms. Indeed, as we leave the land of terror, we limp.

With Trible, we know from these biblical stories that there are certain central characters in our religious heritage whom God did not

43

help and did not rescue, yet whose memory is retained in our tradition exactly because they expose the soft underbelly of our religious and theological claims. The tragedy of the women whose stories Trible tells is that God did not save them from brutalization by religious men. They were brutalized by the mythological heroes whose names we as a religious community invoke in awe in our worship; yet the same heroes have left in their wake the broken lives and shattered dreams of other children of God whose only sin was that they were born the wrong gender or they were too defenseless against the powerful.

It is not only women whose stories of victimization and exploitation are retained in the biblical narrative. The Scriptures also contain texts of terror for men, texts in which the harshest analytical light is thrown upon the bankruptcy of many of our traditionally inherited male assumptions and definitions. There are texts of terror for men that show us the predictable tragic consequences of the way we have been taught to distance ourselves from our wives and children, from other women, from other men, and even from our own selves. There are texts of terror for men that teach us how wrongly we have been conditioned to parent, to use and abuse power over others, to make shambles out of the opportunities of family life and relationships.

These texts inspire terror in men, even those of us who have addressed the women's movement, because neither society nor our religious tradition has as yet provided us with alternative models of how to act and think differently while still understanding ourselves as men. These texts inspire terror in us because they confront us with the realization that so much of what we have been taught about being men is twisted and potentially abusive, and yet we are abandoned and alone in a search to find another, better way to be men, in relationship or as individuals. These texts inspire terror in us because we now know we must change before it is too late, and yet we do not know how. We feel like Abraham, told by God to leave Haran, but not understanding where he was going or what was expected of him; like Noah, facing impending disaster and not knowing whether he would survive; like Moses, leading the generations after him into the wilderness unsure of what terrors he would find there; like Jonah, afraid to let go because he could not comprehend the rules of the new game.

The Text

2 Samuel 13 ¹It so happened that David's son Absalom had a beautiful sister, whose name was Tamar; and David's son Amnon loved her. ²And Amnon was so tormented that he made himself ill because of his sister Tamar; for she was a supple young thing, and from Amnon's point of view, it was puzzling how he might take advantage of her. ³Now Amnon had a favorite cousin, whose name was Jonadab, the son of Shimeah, David's brother; and Jonadab was a very crafty man. ⁴And he said to him, "O son of the king, why are you so haggard morning after morning? Will you not tell me?" Amnon said to him [haltingly], "I love Tamar, my brother Absalom's sister." ⁵Jonadab said to him, "Lie down on your bed, and pretend to be ill; and when your father comes to see you, say to him, 'Let my sister Tamar come and bring me bread to eat, and prepare the food in my sight, that I may see, and eat from her hand'." ⁶So Amnon lay down, and pretended to be ill; and when the king came to see him, Amnon said to the king, "Pray let my sister Tamar come and make a couple of cakes in my sight, that I may see, and eat from her hand."

⁷Then David sent home to Tamar, saying, "Go to your brother Amnon's house, and make something to nourish him." ⁸So Tamar went to her brother Amnon's house, where he was lying down. She took dough, and kneaded it, and made cakes in his sight, and baked the cakes. ⁹She then took the pan and arranged its contents before him, but he refused to eat. Instead Amnon said, "Everyone get out of here." So everyone left. ¹⁰Then Amnon said to Tamar, "Bring the food into the bed-chamber, that I may eat from your hand there." And Tamar took the cakes she had made, and brought them to Amnon her brother, on into the chamber. ¹¹But when she brought them near him to eat, he grabbed hold of her, and said to her, "Come, lie with me, my sister." ¹²She answered him, "No, my brother, do not degrade me; for such a thing is not done in Israel; do not do this shameful deed. ¹³As for me, where could I carry my shame? And as for you, you would be as one of the base fools in Israel. Therefore I pray you, instead, to speak to the king; for he will not withhold me from you." ¹⁴But he would not listen to her pleading, and being stronger than she, he raped her, and laid with her. ¹⁵Then Amnon hated her with very great hatred; so that the hatred with which he hated her was greater than the love with which he had loved her. And Amnon said to her, "Up! Get out!" ¹⁶But she said to him, "Do not add this greater wrong of sending me away to that which you already did to me." But he would not listen to her. ¹⁷He called the young man who served him and said, "Throw this [thing] out of my presence and lock the door after her." ¹⁸Now she was wearing a long robe with sleeves, for thus were the unmarried daughters of the king clad. So his servant threw her out, and locked the door after her.

¹⁹And Tamar put ashes on her head, and rent the long robe which she wore; and she covered her face with her hands, and began to walk away, wailing as she went. ²⁰And her brother Absalom said to her, "Has Amnon your brother been with you? For the time being, keep silent about this, my sister; he is your brother; do not let this thing destroy your heart." So Tamar dwelt, inconsolable, in her brother Absalom's house. ²¹When King David heard of all these things, he was very angry. ²²But Absalom spoke to Amnon neither good nor bad; for Absalom hated Amnon, because he had raped his sister Tamar.

²³After two full years Absalom had sheepshearers at Baal-hazor, which is near Ephraim, and Absalom summoned all the king's sons. ²⁴And Absalom

came to the king, and said, "Behold, your servant has sheepshearers; pray let the king and his servants go with your servant." 25But the king said to Absalom, "No, my son, let not all of us go, lest we be burdensome to you." He pressed him, but he would not agree to go but did give him his blessing. 26Then Absalom said, "If not, pray let my brother Amnon go with us." And the king said to him, "Why should he go with you?" 27But Absalom pressed him, so that [finally] he sent Amnon and all the king's sons with him. 28Then Absalom commanded his young men, "Mark when Amnon's heart is merry with wine, and when I say to you, 'Strike Amnon,' then kill him. Fear not, for have not I myself commanded you? Be courageous and valiant." 29So Absalom's young men did to Amnon as Absalom had commanded. Then all the king's sons arose, and each to a man mounted his mule and fled. 30While they were on the way, tidings came to David, "Absalom has slain all the king's sons, and not one of them is left." 31Then the king arose, and rent his garments, and lay on the earth; and all his servants stood by with their garments rent.

32But Jonadab the son of Shimeah, David's brother, answered and said, "Let not my lord suppose that they have killed all the young men, the king's sons, for Amnon alone is dead, for by the command of Absalom this has been determined from the day of his raping of his sister Tamar. 33Now therefore let not my lord the king so take it to heart as to suppose that all the king's sons are dead; for Amnon alone is dead." 34But Absalom fled. And the young man who kept the watch lifted up his eyes, and looked, and behold, many people were coming by way of the hillside behind him. 35And Jonadab said to the king, "Behold, the king's sons have come; as your servant has said, so it is." 36And as soon as he had finished speaking, behold, the king's sons came, and lifted up their voice and wept; and the king also and all his servant wept very bitterly. 37But Absalom fled, and went to Talmai the son of Ammihud, king of Geshur. And David mourned for his son day after day. 38So Absalom fled, and went to Geshur and was there three years. 39And the king wished to go out to Absalom; for he was comforted concerning Amnon who had died.

2 Samuel 14 1Now Joab the son of Zeruah perceived that the king's heart turned toward Absalom. 2Joab sent to Tekoa, and fetched from there a wise woman, and said to her, "Pretend to be a mourner, and put on mourning garments; do not anoint yourself with oil, but behave like a woman who has been mourning many days for the dead; 3and go to the king, and speak to him in this manner." So Joab filled her mouth with words. 4When the woman of Tekoa came to the king, she fell on her face to the ground, and bowed low, and said, "Help, O king." 5And the king said to her, "What do you want?" She answered, "Alas, I am a widow woman; my husband is dead. 6And your handmaid had two sons, and they quarreled with one another in the field; there was no one to part them, and one struck the other and killed him. 7Now the whole family has risen against your handmaid, and they say, 'Give up the man who struck his brother, that we may put him to death for the life of his brother whom he murdered and we will destroy the heir also.' Thus they would quench my last living ember, and leave to my husband neither name nor remnant upon the face of the earth." 8Then the king said to the woman, "Go to your house, and I will give orders concerning you." 9The woman of Tekoa said to the king, "On me be the sin, my lord the king, and on my father's house; let the king and his throne be guiltless." 10The king said, "If any one says anything to you, bring him to me, and he shall never touch you again." [11]Then she said, "Pray let the king remember the Lord your God, that the avenger of blood slay no more, lest my son be destroyed." He said, "As the Lord lives, not one hair of your son's shall fall to the ground."

[12]Then the woman said, "Pray let your handmaid speak a word to my lord the king." He said, "Speak." [13]And the woman said, "Why then have you perpetrated such a thing against the people of God? The king speaks this thing as one who is guilty, inasmuch as the king does not bring home again his banished one. [14][A parable:] We must all die, we are like water split on the ground, which cannot be gathered up again; neither does God take away life, but instead devises means whereby none of us remain banished from him. [15]Now I have come to say this to my lord the king because the people have made me afraid; and your handmaid thought, 'I will speak to the king; it may be that the king will perform the request of his servant. [16]For the king will hear, to deliver his handmaid from the hand of the one who would destroy me and my son together from the inheritance of God.' [17]And your handmaid thought, 'Let the word of my lord the king be a comfort'; for as an angel of God, so is my lord the king to discern between good and evil. The Lord your God be with you!"

[18]Then the king answered the woman, "Do not conceal from me what I am about to ask you." And the woman said, "Let my lord the king speak." [19]The king said, "Is the hand of Joab with you in all this?" The woman answered and said, "As surely as you live, my lord the king, one cannot turn to the right hand or to the left from anything that my lord the king has said. It was your servant Joab who commanded me; it was he who put all these words in the mouth of your handmaid. [20]In order to change the course of affairs your servant Joab did this. But my lord is wise like the wisdom of an angel of God to know all things that are on the earth." [21]Then the king said to Joab, "Behold now, I grant this; go, bring back the young man Absalom." [22]And Joab fell on his face to the ground, and bowed low, and thanked the king; and Joab said, "Today your servant knows that I have found favor in your sight, my lord the king, in that the king has granted the request of his servant."

[23]So Joab arose and went to Geshur, and brought Absalom to Jerusalem. [24]And the king said, "Let him dwell apart in his own house, and let him not see my face." So Absalom dwelt apart in his own house, and did not see the face of the king. [25]Now in all Israel there was no one so much to be praised for his beauty as Absalom; from the sole of his foot to the crown of his head there was no blemish in him. [26]And when he shaved his head (at the end of every year he would cut it; it was so heavy on him that he had to), he weighed the hair of his head at two hundred sheqels by the king's weight. [27]There were born to Absalom three sons, and one daughter whose name was Tamar; she was a woman of beautiful appearance.

[28]So Absalom dwelt two full years in Jerusalem, yet not once did he come into the king's presence. [29]Therefore Absalom sent for Joab, to send him to the king; but Joab would not come to him. And he sent a second time, but Joab would not come. [30]Then he said to his servants, "See, Joab's field is next to mine, and he has barley there; go and set it on fire." So Absalom's servants set the field on fire. [31]Then Joab arose and came to Absalom at his house, and said to him, "Why have your servants set my field on fire?" [32]Absalom answered Joab, "Behold, I sent word to you, 'Come here, that I may send you to the king, to ask, "Why have I come

from Geshur? It would be better for me to be there still." Now therefore let
me look into the face of the king; and if there is sin in me, let him kill me."
33Then Joab went to the king, and reported to him; and he summoned
Absalom. So he came to the king, and bowed so low before the king that
his faced touched the ground; and the king kissed Absalom.

2 Samuel 15 1After this, Absalom acquired for himself a chariot and
horses, and fifty men to run before him. 2And Absalom would rise early and
stand beside the way of the gate; and when any one had a suit to come
before the king for judgment, Absalom would call to him, and say, "From
what city are you?" And when he said, "Your servant is of such and such a
tribe in Israel," 3Absalom would say to him, "See, your claims are good and
right; but the king has failed to appoint someone to hear you." 4Absalom
said moreover, "Oh that I were made judge in the land! Then every one
with a suit or cause might come to me, and I would mete out justice." 5And
when anyone came near to bow low before him, he would extend his hand,
and take hold of him, and kiss him. 6Thus Absalom did to all Israel who
came to the king for judgment; so Absalom stole the hearts of the people of
Israel. 7And at the end of forty [i.e., four?] years Absalom said to the king,
"Pray let me go and pay my vow, which I have vowed to the Lord, in
Hebron. 8For your servant vowed a vow while I dwelt at Geshur in Aram,
saying, 'If the Lord will indeed bring me back to Jerusalem, then I will offer
worship to the Lord.' " 9The king said to him, "Go in peace." So he arose,
and went to Hebron. 10But Absalom sent spies throughout all the tribes of
Israel, saying, "As soon as you hear the sound of the shofar, then say
'Absalom is king at Hebron.' " 11With Absalom went two hundred men from
Jerusalem whom he invited; they went in their naivete, knowing nothing.
12And Absalom sent Ahithophel the Gilonite, David's counselor, from his city,
from Giloh, while he offered sacrifices. And the conspiracy grew strong,
and the people with Absalom kept increasing.
   13Then a messenger came to David, saying, "The hearts of the people of
Israel have gone after Absalom." 14David then said to all his servants who
were with him at Jerusalem, "Arise, and let us flee; or else there will be no
escape for us from Absalom; go in haste, lest he overtake us suddenly, and
bring down evil upon us, and smite the city with the edge of the sword."
15The king's servants said to the king, "Behold, your servants are ready to
do whatever my lord the king decides." 16So the king went forth, and all his
household after him on foot. And the king left behind ten women who were
concubines to tend the house. 17And the king went forth, and all the people
after him; and they halted at the last house. 18And all his servants passed
on by him; and all the Cherethites, and all the Pelethites, and all the six
hundred Gittites who had followed him from Gath, passed on in front of the
king. . . . 30But David went up the Ascent of Olives, weeping as he went,
barefoot and with his head covered; and every one of the people who were
with him covered their heads, and they went up, weeping as they went.
31And it was told David, "Ahithophel is among the conspirators with
Absalom." And David said, "O Lord, I pray thee, turn the counsel of
Ahithophel into foolishness."

2 Samuel 16 15Now Absalom and all the people, the people of Israel,
came to Jerusalem, and Ahithophel with him. 16And when Hushai the
Archite, David's friend, came to Absalom, Hushai said to Absalom, "Long
live the king! Long live the king!" 17And Absalom said to Hushai, "Is this

your loyalty to your friend? Why did you not go with your friend?" ¹⁸And Hushai said to Absalom, "No; for whom the Lord and this people and all the people of Israel have chosen, his I will be, and with him I will remain. ¹⁹And again, whom should I serve? Should it not be his son? As I have served your father, so I will serve you." ²⁰Then Absalom said to Ahithophel, "Give your counsel; what shall we do?" ²¹ Ahithophel said to Absalom, "Go in to your father's concubines, whom he has left to keep the house; and all Israel will hear that you have made yourself odious to your father, and the hands of all who are with you will be strengthened." ²²So they pitched a tent for Absalom upon the roof; and Absalom went in to his father's concubines in the sight of all Israel. ²³Now in those days the counsel which Ahithophel gave was as if one consulted the oracle of God; so was all the counsel of Ahithophel esteemed, both by David and by Absalom.

2 Samuel 17 ¹Moreover Ahithophel said to Absalom, "Let me choose twelve thousand men, and I will set out and pursue David tonight. ²I will come upon him while he is weary and discouraged, and throw him into a panic; and all the people who are with him will flee. I will strike down the king only, ³and I will bring all the people back to you as a bride comes home to her husband. You seek the life of only one man; the rest of the people will be unharmed." ⁴And the advice pleased Absalom and all the elders of Israel. . . .

2 Samuel 18 ¹Then David mustered the men who were with him, and set over them commanders of thousands and commanders of hundreds. ²And David sent forth a third of the army under the command of Joab, a third under the command of Abishai the son of Zeruiah, Joab's brother, and a third under the command of Ittai the Gittite. And the king said to the people, "I myself will also go out with you." ³But the people said, "You shall not go out. For if we flee, they will not care about us. If half of us die, they will not care about us, for there are already ten thousand such as we; therefore it is better that you should be our help from the city." ⁴The king said to them, "Whatever seems best to you, I will do." So the king stood at the side of the gate, while all the people marched out by hundreds and by thousands. ⁵And the king ordered Joab and Abishai and Ittai, "Deal gently for my sake with the young man Absalom." And all the people heard when the king gave orders to all the commanders concerning Absalom. ⁶So the people went out into the field against Israel; and the battle was fought in the forest of Ephraim. ⁷And the people of Israel were defeated there by the servants of David, and the slaughter there was great on that day, twenty thousand men.
⁸The battle spread over the face of all the country; and the forest devoured more people that day than the sword. ⁹And Absalom chanced to meet the servants of David. Absalom was riding upon his mule, and the mule went under the thick branches of a great oak, and his head caught fast in the oak, and he was left hanging between heaven and earth, while the mule that was under him went on. ¹⁰And a certain man saw it, and told Joab, "Behold, I saw Absalom hanging in an oak tree."¹¹ Joab said to the man who told him, "What, you saw him? Why then did you not strike him there to the ground? I would have been glad to give you ten pieces of silver and a leather belt." ¹²But the man said to Joab, "Even if I felt in my hand the weight of a thousand pieces of silver, I would not put forth my hand against the king's son; for in our hearing the king commanded you and

Abishai and Ittai, 'For my sake protect the young man Absalom.' ¹³On the other hand, if I had pretended to risk my life (and there is nothing hidden from the king), then you yourself would have stood aloof." ¹⁴Joab said, "I will not waste time like this with you." And he took three darts in his hand, and thrust them into the heart of Absalom, while he was still alive in the midst of the oak. ¹⁵And ten young men, Joab's armor-bearers, surrounded Absalom and struck him, and killed him. ¹⁶Then Joab blew the shofar, and the people returned from pursuing Israel; for Joab restrained them. ¹⁷And they took Absalom, and threw him into a great pit in the forest, and raised over him a very great heap of stones; and all Israel fled every one to his own tent. ¹⁸Now Absalom in his lifetime had taken and set up for himself the pillar which is in the Valley of the King, for he said, "I have no son to keep my name in remembrance"; he called the pillar after his own name, and it is called Absalom's Monument to this day.

¹⁹Then said Ahimaaz the son of Zadok, "Let me run, and bring the news to the king that the Lord has delivered him from the power of his enemies." ²⁰And Joab said to him, "You are not to bear tidings today; you may bear tidings another day, but today you shall bear no tidings, for the king's son is dead." ²¹Then Joab said to the Cushite, "Go, tell the king what you have seen." The Cushite bowed before Joab, and ran. ²²Then Ahimaaz the son of Zadok said again to Joab, "Come what may, let me also run after the Cushite." And Joab said, "Why will you run, my son, seeing that you bear no profitable tidings?" ²³"Come what may," he said, "I will run." So he said to him, "Run." Then Ahimaaz ran by the way of the plain, and outran the Cushite.

²⁴Now David was sitting between the two gates; and the watchman went up to the roof of the gate by the wall, and when he lifted up his eyes and looked, he saw a man running alone. ²⁵And the watchman called out and told the king. And the king said, "If he is alone, there is news in his mouth." And he came nearer and nearer. ²⁶And the watchman saw another man running; and the watchman called down to the gate and said, "See, another man running alone!" The king said, "He also brings news." ²⁷And the watchman said, "It seems to me that the running of the foremost is like the running of Ahimaaz the son of Zadok." And the king said, "He is a good man, and comes with good news." ²⁸Then Ahimaaz cried out to the king, "All is well." And he bowed before the king with his face to the earth, and said, "Blessed be the Lord your God, who has delivered up the men who raised their hand against my lord the king." ²⁹And the king said, "Is it well with the young man Absalom?" Ahimaaz answered, "When Joab sent the king's servant, your servant, I saw a great tumult, but I do not know what happened." ³⁰And the king said, "Turn around, and stand here." So he turned aside, and stood still. ³¹And behold, the Cushite came; and the Cushite said, "Good tidings for my lord the king! For the Lord has delivered you this day from the hand of all who rose up against you." ³²The king said to the Cushite, "Is it well with the young man Absalom?" And the Cushite answered, "May the enemies of my lord the king, and all who rise up against you for evil, be like that young man." [Heb. 19:1] ³³And the king was deeply moved, and went up to the chamber over the gate, and weeping as he went, he said, "O my son Absalom, my son, my son Absalom! Would I had died instead of you, O Absalom, my son, my son!"

Absalom, Defiant Son

The story of Absalom is found in 2 Samuel 13–19. Here, as in so many other places in the Bible, the story is told from the point of view of the historical victor—in this case, of Absalom's father, King David. To address the full impact of these texts of terror for men, we must read between the lines; we must reconstruct the story from the point of view of a character other than the historical victor. The story as we have it in the text carries the ethics, the morality, and the judgments of kings, patriarchs, and fathers, those powerful males who so shaped our scriptural heritage that they could also remove or attempt to silence the voices of their own victims. Absalom defied convention by defending a raped woman against a patriarchy that despised her worth. He turned to his father for justice and love, but found instead rejection and emotional coldness. Yet Absalom's voice is almost silenced by patriarchal censorship of the scriptural text. But any cry for justice by the victimized is not easily silenced for long. With careful reading, the pain of Absalom calls out to us even from behind the curtain of censorship imposed upon the story by cold fathers and powerful kings.

Absalom was the third son born to King David when he was in Hebron, before he became king of the united tribes in Jerusalem. We do not know how many daughters King David had by his various wives, for Scripture is usually not interested in telling the story, or even the names, of many women. Each of David's sons is named in the text, as the child of David's union with such-and-such a bought wife or concubine, but only one daughter is named: Tamar. She is named by the textual censors both because she is so beautiful and because she is ultimately to be shamefully degraded. David's first-born son is Amnon, thus the rightful heir to David's power and wealth. The third-born son is Absalom. Somewhere between the two boys we understand that there was one other son, Chileab, and at least the one daughter whose name we do know. Younger than Amnon and older than Absalom, Tamar is to find herself caught between these two brothers. For Phyllis Trible, this is the beginning of the tragedy of Tamar. Our purpose here is not to focus on Tamar, but on Absalom, her younger brother, soon to become her defender.

The birth of Absalom is mentioned in passing in the genealogy of 2 Sam. 3:3, but Absalom does not appear in the developed scriptural account until he abruptly shows up, as a young man, in chapter 13. "Now Absalom, David's son, had a beautiful sister, whose name was

51

Tamar; and after a time, Amnon, David's son, loved her." We note that all three are siblings, yet Amnon and Absalom are described as sons of David, while Tamar is described as Absalom's sister, but not as Amnon's sister, though indeed she was. From the text we understand that Tamar and Absalom were brother and sister bound together as being both unusually beautiful young adults. Neither of them could inherit, Absalom because he was not first born, and Tamar because she was female. But perhaps they are bound together by a still-deeper sibling bond, for of all David's children, named sons and "unnamed" daughters, it is only Absalom who will come to the defense of Tamar. Tamar and Absalom are close in age and bound in beauty and loyal sibling love for each other. Amnon, the eldest and the heir, desires sexually his beautiful sister Tamar; he lusts for her to the extent that he becomes ill, obsessed with finding a way to lie with the young virgin. Jonadab, cousin of Amnon, and of course cousin too of Tamar and Absalom, devises a scheme wherein Amnon will feign to be sick in bed and will request of their father David that Tamar be commanded to come into Amnon's room to feed and to nurse him. The biblical text makes Amnon's deviousness obvious: when Amnon and Jonadab are plotting, Tamar is called "the sister of my brother Absalom," but when David comes to see his ailing son, Amnon says, "Let *my* sister come to me." In the middle of the young men's plotting, Tamar is a sexual object, unrelated to Amnon; but in the execution of the plot, Amnon realizes that he must convince his father by pretending the natural affection of siblings. Once Tamar is in Amnon's room, Amnon rapes her violently and then, taunting her in her despair and degradation, ejects her from his princely chamber. As she flees distraught from the room, it is Absalom who meets her.

Sensitive, perceiving what has just happened without being told, Absalom says to Tamar: "Has *your* brother lain with you, *my* sister?" (13:20) Note the awkward, peculiar syntax—not *our* brother, *our* sister, but rather "has *your* brother lain with you, *my* sister?" Absalom's distancing from Amnon is already clear. Tamar might wish to continue to claim Amnon as a brother, but Absalom will no longer do so. And then Absalom offers himself to Tamar as her defender: "For the time being (*'attah*), keep this quiet, my dear sister; he is your brother, but do not allow this thing to destroy your heart." Absalom takes Tamar into his own private chambers, where he protects her in her desolation. The tenderness and concern of her brother Absalom contrast sharply with the callous cruelty of her brother Amnon.

At this point, the serious student of Scripture is presented with one of those textual anachronisms that make biblical studies so fascinating: At 13:21, the usual English texts read: "When [the] King, David, heard of all these things, he was very angry." Not "when their father," not just "when David," but when the distant and powerful emperor King David (who happened also to be their father) heard. . . . The statement suggests the reign of patriarchy and power, not the tenderness of paternal love. Yet more interestingly, alternative manuscripts, such as the Greek Septuagint and the Qumran manuscripts, read instead: "When the king heard this, he did not rebuke Amnon, *for he was the first-born son.*"

How did the king hear? We can only guess. Surely it was not from Amnon; would a son tell a father that he had raped his own sister? Surely it was not from Tamar; would a shamed and despairing daughter run to her father, when her devaluation within the patriarchal system was already so clear from the time of her infancy? We might conjecture that the king heard it from Absalom, who in his anger over the act turned to David for redress, having counseled Tamar to bide her time and not let this deed destroy her heart. But what Absalom got was not redress, but rather David "refused to rebuke Amnon, because he was the first-born son." A young and perhaps still naive son appeals to his father for justice and finds instead that his father is "the king," defending the male prerogative to abuse women, even within the family.

The distant father, the powerful king, the monofocal patriarch, defender of the rights of men to use women, the hollow authority of one so powerful and yet who will not upset the family by confronting sexual violence within it—these images by their injustice strike the sensitive reader sharply. So they surely also struck Absalom, for the text tells us that from that day forward, Absalom would not speak to Amnon, "for Absalom hated Amnon, because he had raped Absalom's sister Tamar." Again the contrast: the text states not that Amnon had raped his own sister Tamar, but that Amnon had raped Absalom's sister Tamar. The bond of brother and sister grows tighter as they become isolated from the seat of power in the family, the only power that can confront sexual abuse and yet refuses to do so.

Absalom harbors his hatred for Amnon as well as for his father, for two full years (13:23). At that time, he attempts to use his father David as part of a plot to take revenge on Amnon for the rape of Tamar. But we note that the story indicates Absalom's hatred of his own father, as well as of Amnon: David is never referred to in this section of the story by name, or even as Absalom's own father. Rather the story tells us that Absalom came to "the king" for cooperation. The king is David, Absalom's father, father of Tamar; yet even two years later Absalom seems to refuse to call him father, or even David. King David is now so distanced from his son, by his refusal to effect justice for a despicable crime within the family, that he is simply an impersonal object, an office, "the king," and all Absalom's brothers are simply "the king's sons."

One person, oddly, is referred to by name. We note that in 13:26, Absalom refers, in David's presence, to "*my* brother Amnon." This is the only time in the narrative when Absalom claims kinship to Amnon, and it echoes the use of "my" at 13:6. In both instances, the use of "my" is a glaring ploy to persuade David to cooperate with plotted violence. It becomes obvious that the son Absalom has learned well from his father and others: the pretense of family loyalty is the convenient mask for unchallenged forms of interfamily violence. So Absalom, with the help of his own royal servants, succeeds in getting Amnon drunk and then kills him. David has already proven himself unjust in the eyes of Absalom, so when Amnon is slain, Absalom knows well that he cannot turn to David for any understanding of the propriety of this vengeful act. The king has been unjust before, and he can only be expected to be unjust now. Absalom flees to the home of his maternal grandfather for refuge.

The text then tells us that David mourns "his son" (presumably his son Amnon), every day for three years. Only at the end of this extended time does he seem to remember his son Absalom, still hiding in the home of his maternal grandfather, and begin to wish for some sort of reconciliation. That David mourned Amnon for three times the normative period of mourning, during which time Absalom seems to have heard nothing from his father, cannot have escaped Absalom's notice.

KING DAVID AND ABSALOM

David, Distant Father

Throughout this story there is no mention of Absalom's mother, only of the maternal grandfather and various other males of the story. This is not a multidimensional story about men and women. Rather, it is a skillfully told story about the dysfunctional relationship between a father and a son brought about by the father's emotional distance from his own children. It is a man's story about men, for other than Tamar and the seer of Tekoa there are no women in this extended portion of the David cycle. It is a story about what happens when a father is busy exercising power, when he becomes a caricature of success to his children and when he protects a man's prerogative for traditional male roles, even at the expense of his family. As if this alienation were not already tragic enough, the story continues.

Joab, King David's military commander in chief, believes the time has come for some reconciliation between father and son. He attempts to effect this through the dramatic pretense of a clairvoyant woman from Tekoa, whom he hires to fool King David. David, seeing through the plot, gets the woman to confess that she has acted only at Joab's request. David then says to Joab (14:21) that Joab may bring Absalom back to Jerusalem, not because David desires to see his own son, but rather in order to placate Joab, David's closest business associate. King David himself does not go out to seek reconciliation with his younger son, nor does he make any apparent effort to send a message to Absalom.

Joab brings Absalom from his maternal grandfather's, but sensing that all is not yet well with the king, does not bring Absalom to the royal palace. Hearing that Absalom is in Jerusalem, his father issues an order that Absalom is not to enter the royal palace, but is to dwell elsewhere. The angry son is not to be brought home. Here, perhaps for the first time, we see the father beginning to crumble, for it may be that he knows that if Absalom comes home, he will have to face the truth of how estranged he has become from his own son, as a result of his emotional distance and his refusal to act justly within the system of family sexual abuse. The power is now Absalom's; David's fear of his own son has made him the impotent patriarch. The functioning of traditional male expectations and roles has reached its predictable result: a powerful angry son and a powerless frightened father, who is unable to challenge the expectations of society enough to recover the love and the justice so long ago asked of him.

For two years Absalom waits to see if he will be summoned by his father. Finally he chooses to take the situation into his own hands; it has now been five years since he has seen his father. He decides to call his father's bluff: he will go to David's throne, and if in his heart of hearts David believes he is guilty, he will kill Absalom. On the other hand, if Absalom lives, his father will have admitted his own complicity in the system of family violence. "So Absalom came to the king, and bowed himself on his face to the ground before the king; and the king kissed Absalom" (14:33). Again we note that David has no name. It might be claimed that David's gesture humanizes him again, and yet the text belies our desire to redeem the fabled king. "The king" kissed Absalom. A father does not kiss a son, but an occupation kisses a person. The son, swallowing his pride, comes home to find his father a caricature. The now-named son, by which the seat of true power is indicated, comes before the throne and lives. It is not so much in the kiss, a gesture of the king's apology to Absalom, that the text reveals Absalom's defeat of his own father, but in the fact that David no longer has a name. The opportunity to be simply David and Absalom, father and son, presents itself, and David passes it by. He retreats into his professional role, and Absalom's critique of his father's emotional bankruptcy is proven true. His father has no identity except his professional role. The tender humanity and creative promise of the parent-child relationship has disappeared into the marketplace of economic success and power. Had only David been able to do something very different at this last opportunity for reconciliation, the tragic ending of the story might have been averted.

Absalom, now powerful, beautiful, well-trained in cunning, spends the next four years carefully consolidating his power to overthrow his father. David flees Jerusalem in fear, leaving behind only ten concubines to keep the palace running. Absalom brings his armies to Jerusalem, intending to declare himself king. Seeking a symbol for having displaced his father in authority, Absalom has sex in public with ten concubines left behind (16:20). He has now displaced his father in his father's bed. The sensitive son, protector of the raped

Tamar, has now in his bitterness adopted the same masculine traditional insensitivity and violence toward women that were the cause
of his original estrangement from his family. The story has moved full
circle, from machismo to tenderness to machismo, and no male character in the story is left unvictimized.

Absalom declares war on his father, heading the army himself in
hopes of seeking ultimate revenge on his father by killing him with
his own hands. South of Bethlehem, in the heat of battle, Absalom
rides through the woods. As he passes under a large oak tree, he
somehow gets entangled in the branches and cannot wrench himself
loose. (A later tradition claims that his beautiful, long, curly hair
became entangled, so that the source of his youthful pride and virility
becomes the occasion for his death.) Finding Absalom entangled in
the tree, Joab, David's commander-in-chief and closest business associate who had tried so unsuccessfully six years earlier to reconcile
father and son, now sees that the future is lost to both father and son
and stabs Absalom in the heart. Joab's troops desecrate the body, and
Joab sends messengers—a loyal Israelite named Ahimaaz and an
unnamed black servant—to the king to break the news that his beautiful, once-sensitive and now-bitter, young son is dead. The moving
text from 2 Samuel 18 speaks eloquently for itself:

> [32]The king said to the Cushite, "Is it well with the young man Absalom?"
> And the Cushite answered, "May the enemies of my lord the king, and all
> who rise up against you for evil, be like that young man." [Heb. 19:1] [33]And
> the king was deeply moved, and went up to the chamber over the gate,
> and weeping as he went, he said, "O my son Absalom, my son, my son
> Absalom! Would I had died instead of you, O Absalom, my son, my son!"

Here at last we see the emotion in David that we wish he had shown
so much earlier in the story.

A Text of Terror
for Men

Why do I believe that the story of David and Absalom should be
classified as a text of terror for men? First, because it shows us the
tragic but predictable result of our emotional dysfunction as men, a
dysfunction learned in childhood and reinforced in our professional
lives. With careful reading of the whole text, David can be seen to

have emotions, but he appears unable to share them with Absalom. He cares enough for Amnon to visit him when he is ill, even without being summoned. He kisses Absalom in the palace, though one could almost read this as an empty gesture. At the end of the story he weeps, but it is too late, for both sons are now dead, and neither can see the human David who lay behind the professional office all along.

Second, the story haunts us with the realization that our children are more like us than we want. Absalom's rebellion and cruelty appear to be nothing more than a mirror of his father's character. In addressing the story, we realize that it is not enough simply to create new opportunities for our children, in the hopes that they will seize them. As long as we do not change ourselves, our children will imitate, and ultimately perpetuate, our most negative characteristics and paralyses.

Third, as we identify with the father and king portrayed here, we get a sense of the price we must pay in order to act out the new sensitivity to which we feel called. David's choice seems to have been between nurturing justice and love within his family and turning his energies to the power of the throne. The text is frightening in that it seems to suggest that nurture and professional commitment are mutually exclusive categories and that the perpetuation of the traditional male absorption in work, from which we have learned to draw so much of our sense of who we are, leaves the children in our families victims of illusion and violence.

In his book *Finding Our Fathers: The Unfinished Business of Manhood*, Samuel Osherson writes:

> The search to identify what it means to be a male nurturer, to be a father who cares and protects in a fuller, more engaged way than just by imitating a John Wayne tough guy/soldier or a businessman/breadwinner, is the serious quest that underlies the at times seemingly comic male self-explorations of our times. How to be strong and caring? Those are themes that men are struggling with.
>
> Sitting at lunch with a former Harvard administrator who has just turned forty, I hear about his recent week at a men's retreat north of San Francisco. Of all the activities of those days, one incident stands out for him.
>
> "One of the exercises we did was based on those American Indian initiation ceremonies where the brave has to run a gauntlet composed

of all the men of the tribe." The entire group of fifty men lined up in a gauntlet, and each person ran down it, *holding a doll, an infant.* "The doll was to give us a purpose, we were to shelter it from the blows as we ran."

Enfolding the vulnerable with male strength.

I believe men want to do this, but we do not know how. Christian tradition has given us a distant fatherly God whose nurturing side is rarely acknowledged. Traditional sex-role stereotyping offers virtually no models for "enfolding the vulnerable with male strength." There is as yet no real community of men in which we can learn what it means to nurture each other or to nurture a son. Such communities are only beginning to develop, and while they have begun to address issues of male peer bonding, thus far they have not addressed well the relationship between father and son.

As long as we do not know how to shape nurturing relationships one-to-one, we cannot know how to live in a nurturing community. Yet from its inception, the church has understood itself as a "community of faith." What does the word "community" mean for those who do not know how to nurture relationships? If we are already too isolated from other men, a personal faith is of little hope for offering new sensitivities to God's presence in community. How can we understand a "God who dwells among us" if there is no "us" among whom to dwell? How can we understand a God of both a loving justice and a forgiving mercy when we have been taught by our role-heritage to opt instead for authoritarianism and isolationism within our own families?

CHAPTER · FOUR

The Sins of the Fathers and an Innocent Generation
Abraham and His Son Ishmael

As mentioned in the previous chapter, our received scriptural heritage is shaped by the patriarchal victors of the developing tradition. In the story of David and Absalom, we saw how a father's dysfunction was passed down from one generation to the next, as Absalom moved from sensitivity to machismo, modeling the emotional repression and relationship distancing of his father King David. Another father–son relationship in Scripture that has received little attention from the Christian community, and yet which holds a message of terror for men, has a very different outcome. Absalom, the angry younger son of King David, ultimately acts out his anger on the public stage and dies for it. Ishmael, elder son of Abraham, does not act out, but instead seems to disappear quietly from the story. Surely the treatment he receives from his father Abraham is no worse than the treatment Absalom received from his father David, and yet Ishmael seems to leave only an empty space. Ishmael is truly the victim of male emotional repression and men's inability to respond coherently to women's demands for loyalty and commitment. When Abraham cannot make up his mind about the ethical conduct of love and commitment, it is Ishmael the son who seems to pay the price, even more so than his father.

ABRAHAM AND ISHMAEL

The Text

Genesis 16 ¹Now Sarai, Abram's wife bore him no children, but she did have an Egyptian maid whose name was Hagar. ²Sarai said to Abram, "Behold now, the Lord has prevented me from bearing children; go in to my maid; perhaps I shall acquire children by her." And Abram hearkened to the voice of Sarai. ³So Sarai, Abram's wife, took Hagar the Egyptian, her maid, after Abram had dwelt ten years in the land of Canaan, and gave her to her husband Abram as a wife. ⁴And he went in to Hagar, and she conceived; and when she saw that she had conceived, her mistress became trifling in her estimation. ⁵And Sarai said to Abram, "May my wrong be upon you! I myself gave my maid to your embrace, and when she saw that she had conceived, I became trifling in her estimation. May the Lord judge between you and me!" ⁶But Abram said to Sarai, "Behold, your maid is in your hand; do to her as you please." Then Sarai dealt harshly with her, and she fled from her face. ⁷A messenger of the Lord found her by a spring of water in the wilderness, by the spring on the way to Shur. ⁸And he said, "Hagar, maid of Sarai, where have you come from and where are you going?" She said,"I am fleeing from the face of my mistress Sarai." ⁹The messenger of the Lord said to her, "Return to your mistress, and pretend to submit to her hands." ¹⁰The messenger of the Lord also said to her, "I will so greatly multiply your descendants that they cannot be numbered for multitude." ¹¹And the messenger of the Lord said to her, "Behold, you are with child, and shall bear a son; you shall call his name Ishmael [God hears]; because the Lord has hearkened to your affliction. ¹²He shall be a wild ass of a man, his hand against every one and every one's hand against him; and he shall dwell as a buffer against his own kinspeople." ¹³So she called the name of the Lord who spoke to her, "Divinity of My Vision"; for she said, "Have I not seen here the one who sees me?" ¹⁴Therefore the well was called Beer-lahai-roi [the well of one who sees and lives]; it lies between Kadesh and Bered. ¹⁵And Hagar bore Abram a son; and Abram called the name of his son, whom Hagar bore, Ishmael. Abram was eighty-six years old when Hagar bore Ishmael to Abram.

Genesis 17 ¹When Abram was ninety-nine years old the Lord appeared to Abram, and said to him, "I am El Shaddai; continue walking before me and be perfect." . . . ⁹And God said to Abraham, "As for you, you shall keep my covenant, you and your descendants after you throughout their generations. ¹⁰This is my covenant, which you all shall keep, between me and you and your descendants after you: Every male among you shall be circumcised. ¹¹You shall be circumcised in the flesh of your foreskins, and it shall be a sign of the covenant between me and you. . . . ¹⁵And God said to Abraham, "As for Sarai your wife, you shall not call her name Sarai, but Sarah shall be her name. ¹⁶I will bless her; I will even give you a son by her; I will bless her, and she shall be for the nations; kings of peoples shall issue from her." ¹⁷Then Abraham fell on his face and laughed, and said in his heart, "Shall a child be born to a man who is a hundred years old? Shall Sarah, who is ninety years old, give birth?" ¹⁸And Abraham said to God, "O that Ishmael might live in your sight!" ¹⁹God said, "But Sarah your wife shall bear you a son, and you shall call his name Isaac [he laughs]. I will establish my covenant with him as an everlasting covenant for his descendants after him. ²⁰As for Ishmael, I have heard you; behold, I do bless him and make him fruitful and multiply him exceedingly; he shall father twelve princes, and I will make him a great nation. ²¹But my covenant I will establish with Isaac, whom Sarah shall bear to you at this season next year." ²²When he had finished talking with him, God went up from Abraham. ²³Then Abraham took Ishmael his son and all the slaves that were born in his house or were bought with his money, every male among the people of Abraham's house, and he circumcised the flesh of their foreskins that very day, as God had said to him. ²⁴Abraham was ninety-nine years old when he was circumcised in the flesh of his foreskin. ²⁵And Ishmael his son was thirteen years old when he was circumcised in the flesh of his foreskin. ²⁶That very same day Abraham and his son Ishmael were circumcised; ²⁷and all the men of his house, those born in the house and those bought with money from a stranger, were circumcised with him. . . .

Genesis 21 ¹The Lord visited Sarah as he had said, and the Lord did to Sarah as he had promised. ²And Sarah conceived, and bore Abraham a son in his old age at the season of which God had spoken to him. ³Abraham called the name of his son who was born to him, whom Sarah bore him, Isaac. ⁴And Abraham circumcised his son Isaac when he was eight days old, as God had commanded him. ⁵Abraham was a hundred years old when his son Isaac was born to him. ⁶And Sarah said, "God has made laughter for me; every one who hears will laugh with me." ⁷And she said, "Who would have dared say to Abraham that Sarah would suckle children? Yet I have borne him a son in his old age." ⁸And the child grew, and was weaned; and Abraham made a great feast on the day that Isaac was weaned. ⁹But Sarah saw the son of Hagar the Egyptian, whom she had borne to Abraham, mocking. ¹⁰So she said to Abraham, "Cast out this slave woman with her son; for the son of this slave woman shall not be heir with my son Isaac." ¹¹And the thing was extremely displeasing to Abraham on account of his son. ¹²But God said to Abraham, "Be not displeased because of the lad and because of your slave woman; whatever Sarah says to you, do as she tells you, for through Isaac shall your seed be called. ¹³And I will make a nation of the son of the slave woman also, because he is your seed." ¹⁴So Abraham rose early in the morning, and took bread and a skin of water, and gave it to Hagar, putting it on her shoulder, along with the child, and sent her away. And she departed, and wandered in the wilderness of Beersheba. ¹⁵When the water in the skin was gone, she cast the child under one of the bushes. ¹⁶Then she went, and sat down over against him a good way off, about the distance of a bowshot; for she said, "Let me not see the death of the child." And as she sat over against him, she lifted up her voice and wept. ¹⁷And God heard the voice of the lad; and a messenger of God called to Hagar from heaven, and said to her, "What troubles you, Hagar? Fear not; for God has heard the voice of the lad where he is. ¹⁸Arise, lift up the lad, and hold him fast with your hand; for I will make him a great nation." ¹⁹Then God opened her eyes, and she saw a well of water; and she went, and filled the skin with water, and gave the lad drink. ²⁰And God was with the lad, and he grew up; he lived in the wilderness, and became an archer. ²¹He lived in the wilderness of Paran; and his mother took a wife for him from the land of Egypt. . . .

Genesis 22 ¹After these things God tested Abraham, and said to him, "Abraham!" And he said, "Here am I." ²He said, Take your son, [the one with whom alone you are one], *your only son,* whom you love, Isaac, and go to the land of Moriah, and offer him there as a burnt offering upon one of the mountains of which I shall tell you."

Genesis 25   8And Abraham expired and died in a good old age, a sage and full of years, and he was gathered to his peoples. 9And Isaac and Ishmael his sons buried him in the cave of Makhpela in the field of Ephron the son of Zohar the Hittite, which is before Mamre. . . . 12And these are the generations of Ishmael son of Abraham whom Hagar the Egyptian, handmaid of Sarah, bore to Abraham, 13and these are the names of the sons of Ishmael, by their names, according to their generations: the firstborn of Ishmael, Nebaioth, and Kedar and Adbeel and Mibsam, 14Mishma, Dumah, Maasa, 15Hadad, Tema, Jetur, Naphish, and Kedemah. 16These are they, the children of Ishmael, and these are their names, by their towns, and by their encampments; twelve princes according to their nations. 17And these are the years of the life of Ishmael: a hundred and thirty-seven, and he expired and died, and was gathered to his peoples. 18And they dwelt from Havilah to Shur, as a buffer for Egypt, on your way toward Shur; he wound up to the east of his brothers.

Ishmael, Firstborn Son

While Scripture does not contain much material that pertains overtly to divorce as we know it in our contemporary society, the relationship between Abraham and Ishmael does look in some ways like what happens today in many divorced men's relationships to their children. The story of Ishmael reads like a string of broken promises. And the story of Abraham his father reads like that of a husband and father who did not know how to sort out his competing loyalties and responsibilities to two families.

Some parts of the story are already familiar to us. In Gen. 16:1, we are told that "Sarai, Abram's wife, bore him no children, but she did have an Egyptian maid whose name was Hagar. Sarai said to Abram, 'Behold now, the Lord has prevented me from bearing children; go in to my maid; perhaps I shall acquire children her by.' " Abraham is thus presented to us as a man who has two women in his life. One, Sarah the Hebrew, is married, rich, and free; she is also old and barren. The other, Hagar the Egyptian, is single, poor, and bonded, but she is also young and fertile. These are two very different women in Abraham's life: one young, poor, and unmarried, though indentured, and the other older, wealthy, and his wife of many years. This is not immediately parallel to modern situations of divorce and remarriage, for in the biblical account both women share Abraham's house—one as his wife and one as the servant of his wife. Also, unlike many modern situations, it apparently is Sarah who gives her own servant to Abraham for the express purpose that Abraham will impregnate her, thus increasing Sarah's standing in the community by virtue of having children in the house.

Phyllis Trible, in her book *Texts of Terror*, brilliantly analyzes the relationships among Hagar, Abraham, and Sarah from the point of view of Hagar, the servant woman who was so cruelly used both by Sarah and by Abraham. But there is a great deal to be learned as well from a concentration on the two central men of the story: Ishmael, child of Sarah's Abraham and of Hagar the servant woman, firstborn son of his father and therefore heir apparent to Abraham's wealth and promises, according to all the accepted understandings of society; and Abraham, unable to reconcile the relationship between his two families: Hagar and Ishmael, his "second wife" (so to speak) and his firstborn son; Sarah and Isaac, his "first wife" (so to speak) and his second-born son. Though the details in the scriptural account do not match perfectly, what we have here speaks to a contemporary dilemma: How does a father relate to the children of a previous relationship? And how do the children of a previous relationship relate to a father's come-lately new family?

The tension between Abraham and his first and second families is woven throughout the story. At Gen. 16:15, Ishmael is described as Abraham's son—"And Hagar bore Abram a son; and Abram called the name of *his* son, whom Hagar bore, Ishmael." The son at the moment of birth is claimed by the father in the act of naming, though we note that the name itself had been imparted previously by God to Hagar in the midst of her distress, rather than to Abraham. While we can only guess, Ishmael was surely given a place of acclaim and promise, particularly since at the time of his birth, the text tells us that Abraham was already eighty-six years old. At this moment in the story, Hagar is simply the vehicle of delivery, the woman through whom Abraham gains male progeny and through whom Sarah secures her standing in the community. But Sarah aside, the emphasis is on Ishmael, who belongs to Abraham—a firstborn son with all the rights and privileges promised within a patriarchal society.

Ishmael's ultimate destiny is further suggested in the meeting in the wilderness between Hagar and a mysterious messenger of God

(Gen. 16:7). There Hagar is told that, in spite of Sarah's jealousy over her own barrenness as compared to Hagar's fertility, Ishmael will be the first in a long line of multitudinous descendants. The promise was made because God heard Hagar's cry of affliction over the way she was treated by Sarah. This establishes a link between the terms "messenger of God—promise—descendants," all used in the context of Ishmael's future.

At 17:15, when God comes to Abraham with a new promise of covenant and progeny, Abraham's first thought is obviously of Ishmael. In v. 17, he falls on his face in disbelief of God, questioning. Actually, v. 17 appears to be a later addition, or at least it seems to interrupt the textual flow; the promise is also repeated at v. 19, as though v. 17 hadn't been stated. Instead, note the parallel structure of 17:15, "And God said to Abraham" compared to v. 18, "And Abraham said to God." Here is probably the original text, with vv. 16 and 17 interjected later in order to shift the reader's focus onto this child Isaac, who is to be born later. We might then safely assume that the original narrative structure was v. 15, "And God said to Abraham," followed by v. 18, in which Abraham said to God: "A name change signals that something else is going to change too. I want you to promise me that nothing bad will occur to my dear beloved son Ishmael."

Abraham's first thought, the text tells us, is "Oh that Ishmael might live, might prosper in your sight, might be the heir of this new thing which is coming from you, God." At 17:19-20, God boldly denies Abraham's intercession on behalf of Ishmael. Ishmael is not to be within the covenant relationship promised at 17:9. At first, in the earlier reference, the covenant promised to "you and your descendants" sounds as though it means from Abraham through the seed of Ishmael. At 17:19, God makes it clear that another set of "your descendants" was meant. From the lineage of Sarah will come Isaac, progenitor of kings (17:16); Ishmael will father princes (17:20), and princes certainly are not kings.

But Abraham either does not hear, or does not believe. He knows nothing of some future son from a barren wife; he and Sarah are beyond the child-bearing age, and whatever he thought he heard from God makes so little sense that it does not register, or perhaps registers and is rejected. He does know, however, that here in the present he has his longed-for firstborn son. He seems at this point to become determined that this son will inherit God's promises, even if Abraham has to defy God in order to ensure such inheritance. The argument with God here seems clearly to prefigure Abraham's subsequent argument with God over the inhabitants of Sodom (18:16-33). Perhaps Abraham is so insistent with God about Sodom because he has been denied the victory concerning Ishmael.

Abraham seems to cling to Ishmael. Note the repetition: at 17:23, "his son"; at 17:25, "his son"; at 17:26, "his son." All these are references to Ishmael his son, not to the as-yet-unborn Isaac. Yet nowhere in the passage, when God speaks, does God ever use the formula, "Ishmael, your son" or "you and the descendants of Ishmael your son" in the same way that God uses "Isaac your son" at 22:2. Abraham claims and clings to the special relationship with Ishmael, but God never seems to confirm it. What is more, at 17:20, "your son" is noticeably absent. When God says that the covenant is not for Ishmael but for Isaac, at that particular point the text could have read "As for your son Ishmael . . . ," yet the words "your son" are plainly absent.

But Abraham also makes an even more desperate move. Return to note 17:10-11, where God says to Abraham: "You shall be circumcised in the flesh of your foreskins, and it shall be a sign of the covenant between me and you." There is to be a covenant relationship between God and the seed of a particular person; the public mark that indicates that one is a male within that relationship is circumcision, a sign neither easily mistakable nor easily erased. The text seems almost to imply that if a male is circumcised—any male, especially a male descendant of Abraham—he is to be assumed to be within the covenanted relationship with God. Thus we note at 17:23: "Then Abraham took Ishmael his son and all the slaves born in his house or bought with his money, every male among the people of Abraham's house, and he circumcised the flesh of their foreskins that very day, as God had said to him. Abraham was ninety-nine years old when he was circumcised in the flesh of his foreskin. And Ishmael his son was thirteen years old when he was circumcised in the flesh of his foreskin. That very day Abraham and his son Ishmael were circumcised. . . ."

The text here has a tone of desperation about it. Abraham has already been told in 17:19 that Ishmael will not be the heir of the covenant promises. But Abraham refuses to believe this. He has only one son, and further, one firstborn son. This child must be assured a place in the covenant, whether or not God has said no. So Abraham circumcises his son, and the text repeats it in v. 23, 25, and 26 to be sure that we see how urgent was Abraham's desire to secure a place for Ishmael within the promised covenant. A father is fighting against God to ensure the justice due to his only son.

Abraham, Between Two Families

The story line we are following then skips to chapter 21. Sarah, Abraham's wife, conceives the child promised in chapter 17 to Abraham, and Abraham names the boy Isaac, just as he had named the previous child Ishmael. Now Abraham is caught between two families: Hagar and the son Ishmael, and Sarah and the son Isaac. Judging by her absence from the story for more than four chapters, Hagar seems to mean little to Abraham beyond being the mother of his first and deeply beloved boy. Sarah is Abraham's wife from his youth, now mother of an unexpected second son. Abraham has tried desperately to ensure his first beloved son a place within the covenant relationship with God. God has instead told Abraham that Isaac is the son of the covenant, but it seems that Abraham is not completely convinced. At this point in the Abraham saga, Isaac hardly plays any role except as a foil for the story of the tense relationships among Abraham, Hagar, and Ishmael.

At 21:8, the text reads: "And the child grew, and was weaned; and Abraham made a great feast on the day that Isaac was weaned." Then there appears to be some space in time, perhaps even a few years. At 21:9, the text reads: "But Sarah saw the son of Hagar the Egyptian, whom she had borne to Abraham, mocking." While we cannot be sure of the ages of Ishmael and Isaac here, we do at least remember that Ishmael is born fourteen years before Isaac, so is significantly older. There are a number of other important nuances here as well. The text seems to move temporarily away from Abraham's concerns, shifting instead to the relationship between the two women. Even Ishmael is not named; he is simply "the son of Hagar." And Isaac temporarily disappears from the story altogether. Yet at the same time this seems to be the moment when we as readers are confronted with the conflict that is tearing Abraham apart; he has two families, though he apparently will not be one to reconcile them, for he is not described as being in the middle between the two sides. Rather, the two sides, the two women, are face to face, and Abraham is absent at the moment of crisis. Sarah, the new mother, sees Abraham's firstborn child "mocking," and we somehow understand that the reference is to Isaac, second-born, child of a second though more licit relationship, and we are told that Sarah is extremely displeased.

The word "mocking" or "playing" in Hebrew is interesting and can have a variety of meanings. One meaning, which has considerable authority in the later exegetical tradition, is that Sarah caught the two boys exploring each other sexually, as young boys are wont to do. Another meaning, and here the more poignant one, is that Sarah catches Ishmael "laughing" at Isaac. The sense is a play on words: Isaac's name means "laughter" of a pure and innocent kind, yet Sarah catches Ishmael laughing derisively at Isaac, taunting him and making fun of him. The phrase can even be translated, "Sarah saw Ishmael 'Isaac-ing,' " suggesting that she saw Ishmael usurping the position of the child whom Sarah considered to be the firstborn. Exercising a parent's sense of defensiveness for her own offspring, Sarah demands that Abraham sever his relationship with Hagar and Ishmael so that Ishmael will in no way inherit from Abraham, nor indeed have any continuing effect on Isaac. Sarah demands that Abraham choose between his two families and that Isaac the second-born take the place of Ishmael the firstborn as inheritor of the family properties as well as of the promised place within the covenant.

Abraham's reaction is one of distress. The text says at 21:11, "And the thing was extremely displeasing to Abraham on account of his son." But which of the two boys here is his son? The text, throughout chapter 17 and here into chapter 21, has more often referred to Ishmael the firstborn as "his [Abraham's] son" than to Isaac as "his son." To be clearer, the sentence probably should be read, "And the utterance was extremely displeasing to Abraham on account of his love for his son Ishmael." It would be even more accurate to translate the Hebrew freely as follows: "And Sarah's words frightened Abraham to the depth of his being, for he loved Ishmael very much." The usual English text, "very displeasing," does not capture the horror of the situation conveyed by the Hebrew original. Then oddly, in vv. 12 and 13, God appears to step into the situation in order to side with Sarah and to reassure Abraham that Ishmael will not be completely abandoned by God. It seems probable that these two verses are the clarification of a later editor, for the flow of the text seems calculated to cover up or defuse Abraham's anxiety and to apologize for Abraham's glaring failure to defend his firstborn against the demands of the mother of the second-born. Abraham, the first patriarch of Judaism, here seems so weak that we can easily conjecture that a later editor contrived an explanation for his having failed abysmally in the arena of human justice.

Between the lines one reads Abraham as being so frightened that he becomes paralyzed and cannot make a choice between the two families; so he ultimately acquiesces to Sarah's demands that Ishmael be disinherited and driven away. Here then is the first place we can name the tragedy of the situation from a point of view of contemporary men's studies: a man caught between two families is emotionally unable to resolve the dilemma, so he ends up initiating the alienation of one of his own children in order to alleviate his own emotional paralysis. If Abraham had been able to stand up to Sarah, or if he had been able to conceive some other sort of resolution to this conflict between first family and second family, the story might have turned out differently. But he apparently was not. He was trapped by his own emotional conflict in the situation, and the text attempts to cover up Abraham's failure by having God intervene miraculously at this point.

So, acquiescing, Abraham decides to send away what 21:14 alludes to as "Hagar and the child." Note that from the point of his circumcision at the end of chapter 17, and certainly ever after the birth of Isaac, Ishmael is never called by his name, until his brief mysterious appearance at Abraham's burial. He is also never referred to as Abraham's son. Once, at 21:9, he is called "the son of Hagar the Egyptian." All other references to him are as "the child" or "the lad," though we have already ascertained that he is at least fourteen years old, an age of adult responsibility in his cultural context. But as if this insult were not enough, at 22:2 and 12 young Isaac is referred to by God, speaking to Abraham, as "your son [the one with whom alone you are one], your only son," as though Ishmael had never existed at all. It seems the text is trying to indicate the horrible tragedy of the situation, not only for Hagar, though this certainly is Trible's understanding, but as well for Ishmael. Once bereft of his father and deprived of his inheritance, Ishmael no longer has even enough identity for the text to name him, until long after the rest of the story is told. Biblical scholar David Daube describes this moment—the sending away of Hagar beginning at v. 14—as a "divorce," and thus Ishmael becomes the child of Abraham's divorcing of Hagar. There is to be no further contact between Abraham and Ishmael, apparently for the rest of Abraham's life. As we learn in vv. 20-21, thereafter "Ishmael lived in the wilderness, some place in the area of the Sinai desert, Paran, and became an archer, and his mother arranged that he would marry an Egyptian wife."

Ishmael's connection with the Hebrew people is severed; his descendants are to become the enemies of the Hebrew people, if we understand this part of the story in connection with Gen. 16:12. There, it says, "He shall be a wild ass of a man, his hand against every one and every one's hand against him; and he shall dwell as a buffer against his own kinspeople." Though the Hebrew text here is quite obscure, the meaning seems to be that the descendants of Ishmael will forever be not only the enemy of the Hebrews, but also the tribe that stands in the way of Ishmael's own kinspeople ejecting the Hebrews from their land. Ishmael's banishment from Abraham's house, his disinheritance, his alienation from his father, and his displacement within the covenant relationship in spite of Abraham's desperate application of circumcision all create a permanent bitterness against his own father's second family, a bitterness that is to be passed down for generations without possibility of reconciliation.

Abraham does not part easily from Hagar and his firstborn. The text does not tell us that Abraham argued with Sarah over this act. But it does tell us of Abraham's attempt to be solicitous to Hagar in this heart-breaking situation. At 21:14, we are told that "Abraham rose early in the morning, and took bread and a skin of water, and gave it to Hagar, putting it on her shoulder, along with the child, and sent her away." He seems to be attempting to make sure that Hagar, and perhaps even more so his firstborn, survive this expulsion. If he cannot reconcile his two families, at least he can make some effort to assure the survival of the child of his former "wife." Bread and water here symbolize the basic staples of life. Abraham tries to ensure that Hagar and Ishmael's basic needs will be met until they can get back on their feet.

An unusually sharp contrast between the children of Abraham's two families is presented the reader. Ishmael becomes a wild ass of a man, an archer, and a man of violence; Isaac becomes a shepherd. Ishmael comes to dwell in the wilderness as enemy of all; Isaac comes to dwell in a family, in their home, and eventually produces a large family of his own. Ishmael is never mentioned again until the end of the story. Once he becomes the child of divorce, he ceases to exist as a named historical figure until the burial of his father Abraham. There, suddenly and without explanation, he appears standing by the side of Isaac, as Abraham is interred in the cave of Makhpela, which was originally purchased as Sarah's burial place (see Gen. 25:9). Then he disappears again from the story line. Only his descendants remain named, at 25:13-18, as the tradition emerges of symbolically naming Israel's strongest and most permanent enemies as the descendants of Ishmael. All this, we may conjecture, is not the result of God's repeated intervention in the affairs of the family (though this is the way the editor of Genesis tries to tell the story), but rather is the result of Abraham's inability to reconcile his two families and his failure to defend his first family against the demands of his second family.

This is a frightening, deeply disturbing story, and yet we find in the text no feeling words, with the exception of Gen. 21:11. Nor do we find emotions in chapter 22, in which Abraham hears God call for the ritual sacrifice of Isaac, his "only son." In chapter 17, Abraham argues with God long and hard for Ishmael's place in the covenant; in chapter 22 he acquiesces to God's horrifying demand to sacrifice Isaac without argument. Are we to assume that in killing his love for Ishmael, Abraham lost his ability to love Isaac as well? Is his paralysis so deep that his emotions are lost to him forever? This is a classic example of a text that gains the power to grip us by what is omitted—the emotions—rather than by the overt tension of its story line.

A Text of Terror
for Men

Why should this story be classified as a text of terror for men? First, this is a terrifying text because so many American men recognize themselves in Abraham's paralysis. Divorce, split families, and merged families are realities with which so many men live today. In spite of the bizarre mythology that divorced men flourish, the fact is that men suffer deeply, often in relative silence, and their children suffer as a result. Such men do not know how to love two separate families. Love is an emotion most men claim but often exercise with limited creativity. Many divorced men pretend to love the children of their former marriages from afar, with little regular contact. More men than not stop their financial support of their former families. Some who continue their support believe that paying their financial obligations somehow fulfills their parental responsibility. All of these are forms of emotional paralysis and of a failure to explore creatively the broader possibilities of nonresidential parenting.

In her wise book, *Necessary Losses*, Judith Viorst writes:

> Damaging oedipal victories may occur through a parent's death—"I wanted my mother all to myself, and the next thing I knew my father had a heart attack." They may also occur when parents divorce. Several recent studies indicate that boys are less able than girls to cope with their parents' marital breakup, and that the effects on them—which include lowered scholastic achievement, depression, anger, diminished self-esteem, increased drug and alcohol use—are longer lasting and more intense. These studies also suggest that oedipal issues in part explain the greater problems that boys seem to have with divorce.

According to Linda Bird Francke's article "The Sons of Divorce," the mother still winds up with custody of the children—by agreement or by default—more than 90 percent of the time. Thus, when the child is a son, most mothers get the son—and the son gets the mother. "The oedipal conflict is supposed to be resolved in favor of the parent, not in favor of the child," says child psychiatrist Gordon Livingston, whose clinic in Maryland annually sees as many as five hundred children of divorce. "Yet repeatedly, now, it's happening the other way." With the son replacing his father in bed (sometimes quite literally), the ensuing sexual tension and guilt can lead to inner turmoil and troubled behavior. This boy, like Ishmael, too often turns out to be "a wild ass of a man," with hand against brother, dwelling in an emotional wilderness and never welcomed home until it is too late.

A second reason this is a text of terror for men, at least those of us who strive for faith, is that Abraham seems forced to fight God for what seemed to be something predictable and just—his son's right to be his son and to inherit Abraham's wealth. Fighting God is terrifying, for if men have to fight God, then God is not the God we thought we knew. God in such tales of terror is someone mysterious, shadowy, and threatening. We may be reminded of the story of Abraham's grandson Jacob, who in Gen. 32:23 wrestles with a terrifying stranger all night long, till daybreak, and when the stranger "saw that he could not get the better of Jacob, he struck him in the hollow of his thigh, high up near his genitals, so that Jacob's hip was dislocated as they wrestled." We hear the terror in the Jacob story, we feel it viscerally, and we sense the desperation in Abraham's wrestling with God for the future of Ishmael. No man emerges whole, and neither God nor father is what we wanted him to be.

A third reason that this is a text of terror for men is that it teaches the hard lesson of our temptations, as fathers, to prefer one child over another. My mentor Zev Gotthold has pointed out that this is just one of several stories in the Hebrew Bible in which a tragic end is the result of a father's preferential treatment of one child over another. Such stories include not only Abraham and Ishmael, but also Isaac and Esau, and Jacob and Joseph. Interestingly, such a sequence names all three patriarchs, the "fathers" in whose name we invoke our faith. Neither Isaac, in relation to Esau, nor Jacob, in relation to Joseph, seems to learn from the dysfunction of the generation before. The same troubled patterns of fathering are passed through generations, the cycle unbroken. Learning to father differently is hard for men. There are too few models, and even when models exist, we prefer to go it alone, and make our own mistakes. But too often, the mistakes are a repetition of the generations before us.

Finally, we understand this as a text of terror for men because of God's miraculous intervention. Though I have identified Gen. 21:12-13 as a possible later editorial addition in order to cover Abraham's failure, it is nevertheless a frightening addition. By stepping in to cover Abraham's failure, God also seems to change the rules. In the snap of a finger, the heir is disinherited, and a second son put in his place. Abraham's struggle for his son's rights and future security (surely the natural instinct of a father) is derailed by God's stepping in to say, "Now we will do it my way." Men like rules. That is why men are kings, senators, and judges. Boys are told growing up that if they play by the rules, they will succeed. Fathers counsel their sons to avoid sudden career shifts, to conform, to dress for success, to express emotions in certain situations, and to play "the game," whatever it is. Watch a young boy react to another who is cheating; it helps one understand how angry it makes boys, and then later men, when someone fails to follow the rules. Guarding the rules is one way in which men continue to control the echelons of upper-level management: we may admit women, but if we fail to teach them the rules, we can be assured that women cannot compete and succeed.

In this story, God obviously plays by a different set of rules. Some men may react by saying: "If I don't know the rules, how will I know what I'm supposed to do? If I don't know the rules, how will I know whether I'm succeeding? Since like most men, my primary identity is my occupational identity, and I can't tell whether I'm succeeding, how will I know who I am?" We've heard it before—my ways are not your ways, says the Lord—but like Abraham arguing with God, we men don't want to believe that we have misunderstood God's rules, or worse, that God is arbitrary and capricious—that God has no rules. And we are scared.

CHAPTER · FIVE

A Love Surpassing the Love of Women?
Jonathan and David

O ne of the most troubling challenges for men who seek to become more sensitive is to explore new models and functions of male-male friendship. Repeated studies of male friendship patterns suggest that adult males have few, if any, intimate friends of either sex. When men do identify someone as a close friend, it tends to be one of only two types: (1) their wife or (2) their best male friend from a number of years before whom they no longer see regularly. Both possible categories have inherent problems. We live with a continuing high divorce rate. When a man's only friend is his wife, a divorce means loss of his entire support system during the traumatic period in which he most needs support. As for the other category, when men are asked to name their best male friend they often name someone they haven't seen for years, but remember fondly. Of course it is impossible for anyone to be truly in touch with someone they do not see regularly. These so-called "friendships" do not bear the marks of commitment or the melding of personalities. The primary difficulty in male-male friendship is how to handle the scary potential for intimacy, combined with the general male mistrust of making oneself vulnerable by telling the whole truth.

The Hebrew Scriptures contain only two examples of male-male friendship: Job and his friends, and David and Jonathan. The first example is an odd one, in that Job's relationship with his friends contains more accusation, misunderstanding, and mistrust than most men would choose to build into their relationships. But the story of David and Jonathan presents a model that has been often misinterpreted, for reasons largely related to the Hebrew text itself. A closer examination of the text suggests a friendship model of great antiquity. In order to examine this somewhat troubling and misunderstood text, we need to free ourselves of all prior conceptions concerning its possible sexual content and, instead, read it plainly and simply. After that, we will address why the model presented here is frightening for men at the same time that it offers a unique opportunity for growth in relationship commitment and mature sensitivity, if we can only conquer our fear.

The Text

1 Samuel 13 ¹Saul was . . . years old when he began to reign; and he reigned . . . two years over Israel. ²Saul chose three thousand men of Israel; two thousand were with Saul in Michmash and the hill country of Bethel, and a thousand were with Jonathan in Gibeah of Benjamin; the rest of the people he sent every man to his tent. ³Jonathan smote the garrison of the Philistines which was at Geba; and the Philistines heard of it. . . . ¹³And Samuel said to Saul, "You have done foolishly; you have not kept the commandment of the Lord your God, which he commanded you; for now the Lord would have established your kingdom over Israel for ever. ¹⁴But now your kingdom shall not endure; the Lord has sought out a man after his own heart; and the Lord has appointed him to be prince over his people, because you have not kept what the Lord God commanded you." . . . ¹⁶And Saul, and Jonathan his son, and the people who were present with them, stayed in Geba of Benjamin; but the Philistines encamped in Michmash. . . . ¹⁹Now there was no smith to be found throughout all the land of Israel; for the Philistines said, "Lest the Hebrews make themselves a sword or a spear"; ²⁰but every one of the Israelites went down to the Philistines to sharpen his plowshare, his mattock, his axe, or his sickle; ²¹and the charge was a pim for the plowshares and for the mattocks, and a third of a sheqel for sharpening the axes and for setting the goads. ²²So on the day of the battle there was neither sword nor spear found in the hand of any of the people with Saul and Jonathan; but Saul and Jonathan his son had them. ²³And the garrison of the Philistines went out to the pass of Michmash.

1 Samuel 14 ¹One day Jonathan the son of Saul said to the young man who bore his armor, "Come let us go over to the Philistine garrison on yonder side." But he did not tell his father. ²Saul was sitting in the outskirts of Gibeah under the pomegranate tree which is at Migron; the people who were with him were about six hundred men, ³ . . . And the people did not know that Jonathan had gone. ⁴Between the passes by which Jonathan sought to go over to the Philistine garrison, there was a rocky crag on the one side and a rocky crag on the other side; the name of the one was Bozez, and the name of the other Seneh. ⁵The one crag rose on the north in front of Michmash, and the other on the south in front of Geba. ⁶And Jonathan said to the young man who bore his armor, "Come let us go over to the garrison of those uncircumcised; it may be that the Lord will work for us; for nothing can hinder the Lord from saving by many or by few." ⁷And his armor-bearer said to him, "Do all that is in your heart. Turn; I am with you, as in your heart." ⁸Then said Jonathan, "Behold, we will cross over to the men, and we will reveal ourselves to them. ⁹If they say to us, 'Wait until we come to you,' then we will stand still in our place, and we will not go up to them. ¹⁰But if they say, 'Come up to us,' then we will go up; for the Lord has given them into our hand." . . .

¹²And the men of the garrison hailed Jonathan and his armor-bearer, and said, "Come up to us, and we will show you something." And Jonathan said to his armor-bearer, "Come up after me; for the Lord has given them into the hand of Israel." ¹³Then Jonathan climbed up on his hands and feet, and his armor-bearer after him. And they fell before Jonathan, and his armor-bearer killed them after him; ¹⁴and that first slaughter, which Jonathan and his armor-bearer made, was of about twenty men within as it were half a furrow's length which a yoke of oxen might plow. ¹⁵And there was a trembling in the camp, in the field, and among all the people. . . .

¹⁶And the watchmen of Saul in Gibeah of Benjamin looked; and behold, the multitude was surging hither and thither. ¹⁷Then Saul said to the people who were with him, "Number and see who has gone from us." And when they had numbered, behold, Jonathan and his armor-bearer were not there. ¹⁸And Saul said to Ahijah, "Bring the ark of God here." For the ark of God went at that time with the children of Israel. ¹⁹And while Saul was talking to the priest, the tumult in the camp of the Philistines increased more and more; and Saul said to the priest, "Withdraw your hand." ²⁰Then Saul and all the people who were with him rallied and went into the battle; and behold every man's sword was against his fellow, and there was very great confusion. . . .

²³So the Lord delivered Israel that day; and the battle passed beyond Bethaven. ²⁴And the men of Israel were distressed that day; for Saul laid an oath on the people, saying, "Cursed be the man who eats any food until evening, that I may be avenged on my enemies." So none of the people tasted food. ²⁵And all the people [land] came into the forest; and there was honey on the ground. ²⁶And when the people entered the forest, behold the honey was dripping, but no one put his hand to his mouth; for the people feared the oath. ²⁷But Jonathan had not heard his father charge the people with the oath; so he put forth the tip of the staff that was in his hand, and dipped it in the honeycomb, and put his hand to his mouth; and his eyes became bright. ²⁸Then one of the people said, "Your father strictly charged the people with an oath, saying 'Cursed be the man who eats food this day.' " And the people were faint. ²⁹Then Jonathan said, "My father has troubled the land; see how my eyes have become bright, because I tasted a little of this honey. ³⁰How much better if the people had eaten freely today of the spoil of their enemies which they found; for now the slaughter among the Philistines has not been great." . . .

³⁷And Saul inquired of God, "Shall I go down after the Philistines? Wilt thou give them into the hand of Israel?" But he did not answer him that day. ³⁸And Saul said, "Draw near, all you leaders of the people; and know and

see how this sin has arisen today. ³⁹For as the Lord lives who saves Israel, though it be in Jonathan my son, he shall surely die." But there was not a man among all the people that answered him. ⁴⁰Then he said to all Israel, "You shall be on one side, and I and Jonathan my son will be on the other side." And the people said to Saul, "Do what seems good to you." ⁴¹Saul said to the Lord, the God of Israel, "Let it be Thummim." Jonathan and Saul were picked, and the people fled. ⁴²Then Saul said, "Cast lots between me and my son Jonathan." And Jonathan was picked. ⁴³Then Saul said to Jonathan, "Tell me what you have done." And Jonathan told him, saying, "I tasted the taste of a little honey with the tip of the staff that was in my hand; and lo, I must die." ⁴⁴ And Saul said, "God do so and even more; you shall surely die, Jonathan." ⁴⁵Then the people said to Saul, "Shall Jonathan die, who has wrought this great salvation in Israel? Far from it! As the Lord lives, not one hair of his head shall fall to the ground; for God was on his side this day." So the people rescued Jonathan, and he did not die. ⁴⁶Then Saul went up from pursuing the Philistines; and the Philistines went to their own place. . . .

⁴⁹Now the sons of Saul were Jonathan, Ishvi, and Malchishua; and the names of his two daughters were these: the name of the first born was Merav, and the name of the younger Michal; ⁵⁰and the name of Saul's wife was Ahinoam the daughter of Ahimaaz. And the name of the commander of his army was Abner the son of Ner, Saul's uncle; ⁵¹Kish was the father of Saul, and Ner the father of Abner was the son of Abiel. . . .

1 Samuel 17 ⁵⁵When Saul saw David go forth against [Goliath] the Philistine, he said to Abner, the commander of the army, "Abner, whose son is this youth?" And Abner said, "As your soul lives, O king, I cannot tell." ⁵⁶And the king said, "Inquire whose son the stripling is." ⁵⁷And as David returned from slaying the Philistine, Abner took him, and brought him before Saul with the head of the Philistine in his hand. ⁵⁸And Saul said to him, "Whose son are you, young man?" And David answered, "I am the son of your servant Jesse the Bethlehemite."

1 Samuel 18 ¹When he had finished speaking to Saul, the soul of Jonathan was knotted to the soul of David, and Jonathan loved him as his own soul. ²And Saul took him that day, and would not let him return to his father's house. ³Then Jonathan and David made a covenant, because he loved him as his own soul. ⁴And Jonathan stripped himself of the robe that was upon him, and gave it to David, and his armor, and even his sword and his bow and his belt. ⁵And David went out to do whatever Saul sent him, and he succeeded, so that Saul set him over the men of war. And this was good in the sight of all the people and also in the sight of Saul's servants. . . . ⁷And the women sang antiphonally as they made dance, "Saul has slain his thousands, and David his ten thousands." ⁸And Saul was very angry, and this saying displeased him; he said, "They have ascribed to David ten thousands, and to me they have ascribed thousands; and what can he have more but the kingdom?" ⁹And Saul eyed David suspiciously from that day on. . . . ¹⁷Then Saul said to David, "Here is my elder daughter Merav. . . . ²⁰Now Michal Saul's daughter loved David. . . . ²⁸But when Saul saw and knew that the Lord was with David, and that Michal his daughter loved him, ²⁹Saul was still more afraid of David. So Saul was David's enemy continually. . . .

JONATHAN AND DAVID

1 Samuel 19 ¹And Saul spoke to Jonathan his son and to all his servants, that they should kill David. But Jonathan, Saul's son, delighted deeply in David. ²And Jonathan told David, saying, "Saul my father has requested that you be killed; guard yourself in the morning, stay in a secret place and hide yourself; ³and I will go out and stand beside my father in the field where you are, and I will speak to my father about you; I will see what's going on and I will tell you." ⁴Jonathan spoke well of David to Saul his father, and said to him, "Let not the king sin against his servant, against David; because he has not sinned against you, and because his deeds have been very good for you; ⁵for he took his life in his hand and he slew the Philistine, and the Lord performed a great salvation for all Israel. You saw it, and rejoiced; why then will you sin against innocent blood by killing David without cause?" ⁶So Saul hearkened to the voice of Jonathan; Saul swore, "As the Lord lives, he shall not be put to death." ⁷And Jonathan called David, and Jonathan told him all these things. And Jonathan brought David to Saul, and he was in his presence as in days past. ⁸But there was war again; and David went out and fought with the Philistines, and slew them with a smashing blow, so that they fled before him. ⁹Then an evil spirit came from the Lord upon Saul, as he sat in his house with his spear in his hand; [while David played soft music]. ¹⁰Then Saul sought to pin David to the wall with the spear; but he eluded Saul, so that he stuck the spear into the wall. And David fled, and escaped that night. . . .

1 Samuel 20 ¹David fled from Nayot in Ramah, and came and said before Jonathan, "What have I done? What is my crime? What is my sin before your father, that he seeks my soul?" ²And he said to him, "Far from it! You shall not die. Behold, my father does nothing either great or small without revealing it to my ears; why should my father hide this from me? It is not so." ³But David swore again, saying, "Your father knows very well that I have found pleasure in your eyes; and he thinks, 'Let not Jonathan know this, lest he be grieved.' But truly, as the Lord lives and as your soul lives, there is but a step between me and death." ⁴Then Jonathan said to David, "Whatever your soul desires, I will do for you." ⁵David said to Jonathan, "Behold tomorrow is the new moon, and I should not fail to sit beside the king at the ritual meal; but let me go, that I may hide myself in the field till the day after tomorrow. ⁶If your father misses me at all, then say, 'David earnestly asked leave of me to rush to Bethlehem his city; for there is a yearly sacrifice there for all the family.' ⁷If he says, 'Good!,' it will be well with your servant; but if he is very angry, then know that evil is determined by him. ⁸Therefore deal loyally with your servant, for you have brought your servant into a Lord's-covenant with you. But if there is rebelliousness in me, kill me yourself; for why should you bring me to your father?"

⁹And Jonathan said, "Far be it from you! If I knew for sure that it was determined by my father that evil should come upon you, would I not tell you?" ¹⁰Then said David to Jonathan, "But who will tell me if your father responds to you harshly?" ¹¹And Jonathan said to David, "Come, let us go out into the field." So they both went out into the field. ¹²Jonathan swore to David, "The Lord, the God of Israel! When I have sounded out my father, about this time tomorrow, or the third day, behold, if he is well disposed toward David, shall I not then send to you and reveal it to your ears? ¹³The Lord do so to Jonathan and more also; but should it please my father to do you harm, then I will let you know, and send you away, that you may go safely. May the Lord be with you, as he has been with my father. ¹⁴While I

am still alive, make the faithful love of the Lord with me, that I may not die. ¹⁵Do not cut off your loyalty from my house for ever. When the Lord cuts off every one of the enemies of David from the face of the earth, ¹⁶let not the name of Jonathan be cut off from the house of David. And may the Lord take vengeance on David's enemies." ¹⁷And Jonathan asked David to swear his love for him again; for he loved him as he loved his own soul. ¹⁸Then Jonathan said to him, "Tomorrow is the new moon; and you will be missed, because your seat will be empty. ¹⁹And on the third day you will be greatly missed; then come to the place where you hid yourself on the day of the deed, and sit beside the stone Ezel. ²⁰And I will shoot three arrows to the side of it, as though I shot at a mark. ²¹And behold, I will send a lad, saying, 'Go, find the arrows.' If I expressly say to the lad, 'Look, the arrows are on this side of you, take them,' then you are to come, for it is safe for you and there is nothing to fear, as the Lord lives. ²²But if I say to the youth, 'Look, the arrows are beyond you,' then go; for the Lord has sent you away. ²³And as for the pledge which both you and I exchanged, behold, the Lord is between you and me for ever."

²⁴So David hid himself in the field; and when the new moon came, the king sat down to eat the ritual meal. ²⁵The king sat upon his seat, as at other times, upon a seat by the wall; Jonathan stood up, and Abner sat by Saul's side, but David's place was empty. ²⁶Saul did not say anything that day; for he thought, "He has had a wet dream. He is not clean; that's it, he is not clean." [Deut. 23:10] ²⁷But on the second day, the morrow after the new moon, David's place was empty. And Saul said to Jonathan his son, "Why has the son of Jesse not come, either yesterday or today, to the meal?" ²⁸Jonathan answered Saul, "David earnestly asked leave of me to go to Bethlehem; ²⁹he said, 'Let me go; for our family holds a sacrifice in the city, and my brother has ordered me to come. So now, if I have found pleasure in your eyes, let me get away, and see my brothers.' For this reason he has not come to the king's table." ³⁰Then Saul's anger burned against Jonathan, and he said to him, "You son of a perverse, rebellious woman, do I not know that you have chosen the son of Jesse to your own shame, and to the shame of your mother's nakedness? ³¹For as long as the son of Jesse lives upon the earth, neither you nor your kingdom shall be established. Therefore send and fetch him to me, for he is as good as dead." ³²Then Jonathan answered Saul his father, "Why should he be put to death? What has he done?" ³³But Saul cast his spear at him to smite him; so Jonathan knew that his father was determined to put David to death. ³⁴And Jonathan rose from the table in fierce anger and ate no food the second day of the new month, for he was grieved for David, and because his father had humiliated him.

³⁵In the morning Jonathan went out into the field to his appointment with David, and with him a little lad. ³⁶And he said to his lad, "Run and find the arrows which I shoot." As the lad ran, he shot an arrow beyond him. ³⁷And when the lad came to the place of the arrow which Jonathan had shot, Jonathan called after the lad and said, "Is not the arrow beyond you?" ³⁸And Jonathan called after the lad, "Come on, hurry up, don't stand around." So Jonathan's lad gathered up the arrows, and came to his master. ³⁹But the lad knew nothing; only Jonathan and David knew the matter. ⁴⁰And Jonathan gave his weapons to his lad, and said to him, "Go, carry them to the city." ⁴¹And as soon as the lad had gone, David rose from beside the stone heap and fell on his face to the ground, and bowed three times; and they kissed one another, and wept with one another, until David's

JONATHAN AND DAVID

grief exceeded even Jonathan's. ⁴²Then Jonathan said to David, "Go in peace, seeing that we have sworn both of us in the name of the Lord, saying, 'The Lord shall be between me and you, and between my descendants and your descendants, for ever.' " [Heb. 21:1] And he rose and departed; and Jonathan went into the city. . . .

1 Samuel 31 ¹Now the Philistines fought against Israel; and the men of Israel fled before the Philistines, leaving their slain on the slopes of Mount Gilboa. ²And the Philistines overtook Saul and his sons; and the Philistines slew Jonathan and Abinadab and Malchishua, the sons of Saul. The battle went hard for Saul, and the archers found him; and he was mortally wounded by the archers. ⁴Then Saul said to his armor-bearer, "Draw your sword, and thrust me through with it, lest these uncircumcised come and thrust me through, and make sport of me." But his armor-bearer would not, for he was terrified. Therefore Saul took his own sword, and fell upon it. ⁵And when his armor-bearer saw that Saul was dead, he also fell upon his sword and died with him. ⁶Thus Saul died, and his three sons, and his armor-bearer, and all his men, on the same day together. ⁷And when the men of Israel who were on the other side of the valley and those beyond the Jordan saw that the men of Israel had fled and that Saul and his sons were dead, they forsook their cities and fled; and the Philistines came and settled in them. ⁸On the morrow, when the Philistines came to strip the slain, they found Saul and his three sons fallen on Mount Gilboa. ⁹And they cut off his head, and stripped off his armor, and sent messengers throughout the land of the Philistines, to proclaim the good news to the house of their idols and to the people. ¹⁰They put his armor in the temple of Ashtaroth; and they fastened his body to the wall of Beit Shean. ¹¹But when the inhabitants of Jabesh-gilead heard what the Philistines had done to Saul, ¹²all the warriors arose, and journeyed all night, and took the body of Saul and the bodies of his sons from the wall of Beit Shean; and they came to Jabesh and burnt them there. ¹³And they took their bones, and buried them under the tamarisk tree in Jabesh, and fasted seven days.

2 Samuel 1 ¹After the death of Saul, when David had returned from the slaughter of the Amalekites, David remained two days in Ziklag; ²and on the third day, behold, a man came from Saul's camp, with his clothes rent and dirt upon his head. And when he came to David, he fell to the ground and did obeisance. ³David said to him, "Where do you come from?" And he said to him, "I have escaped from the camp of Israel." ⁴And David said to him, "How did it go? Tell me." And he answered, "The people have fled from the battle, and many of the people also have fallen and are dead; and Saul and his son Jonathan are also dead." ⁵Then David said to the young man who told him, "How do you know that Saul and his son Jonathan are dead?" ⁶The young man who told him said, "By chance I happened to be on Mount Gilboa; and there was Saul leaning upon his spear; and lo, the chariots and the horsemen were close upon him. ⁷When he looked behind him, he saw me, and called to me. And I answered, 'Here I am.' ⁸He said to me, 'Who are you?' I answered, 'I am an Amalekite.' ⁹And he said to me, 'Stand over me and kill me; for the throes of death have seized me, and yet my life lingers.' [Compare 1 Sam. 31:4] ¹⁰So I stood over him, and killed him, because I knew that he could not live after he had fallen; and I took the crown which was on his head and the armlet which was on his arm, and I have brought them here to my lord." ¹¹Then David took hold of his clothes, and rent them; and so did all the men who were with him; ¹²and they mourned and wept and fasted until evening for Saul and for Jonathan his son and for the people of the Lord and for the house of Israel, because they had fallen by the sword. ¹³And David said to the young man who told him, "Where did you come from?" And he answered, "I am the son of a sojourner, an Amalekite." ¹⁴David said to him, "How is it you were not afraid to put forth your hand to slaughter the Lord's anointed?" ¹⁵Then David called one of the young men and said, "Go, fall upon him." And he struck him so that he died. ¹⁶And David said to him, "Your blood be upon your head; for your own mouth has testified against you, saying, 'I have killed the Lord's anointed one.'" ¹⁷Then David lamented this lamentation over Saul and Jonathan his son, ¹⁸and he said (To teach the children of Judah the use of the bow; behold it is written in the Book of Jashar): ¹⁹"O young buck of Israel, you lie shattered on your back in death! How the mighty have fallen! ²⁰Tell it not in Gath, proclaim it not in the streets of Ashkelon; lest the Philistine women rejoice, lest the daughters of the uncircumcised dance in triumph. ²¹Mountains of Gilboa, may no dew or rain fall upon you henceforth, nor fields produce grain for sacrificial offerings. For there the shield of the warrior lies cast away in disgrace, he who was the loyal defender of Saul, yet never received the kingly anointing with oil. ²²The bow of brave Jonathan never held back from the blood of the enemy; from the flesh of the powerful, the sword of Saul never returned empty to the scabbard. ²³Beloved Saul and beautiful Jonathan! Neither in life and nor in death were they parted. They were swifter than eagles, they were stronger than lions. ²⁴O daughters of Israel, weep for Saul, who clothed you in scarlet and rich embroideries, who provided ornaments of gold for you to sew upon your apparel. ²⁵How the warriors are fallen in the midst of battle! My Jonathan lies shattered on his back in death. ²⁶I ache for you, Jonathan, my dear brother; you have been so deeply beloved by me, and your love for me was so wonderful, far surpassing the love of women. ²⁷Fallen, fallen are the mighty warriors, and our weapons of war have been brought down to nothing!"

Jonathan and David's Friendship

When Jonathan first appears in the Bible at 1 Sam. 13:3 he is already a young man, probably in his late teens or early twenties, and in command of a large company of soldiers in the battle against the Philistines, the sea-people of the Mediterranean coast southwest of Jerusalem. Most scholars assume that Jonathan had already proven his military prowess in a military campaign against the Ammonites, as documented in 1 Samuel 11, although he is not mentioned in the biblical account of any of those battles. At 13:16 it is suggested that Jonathan is a military commander-in-chief for his father, King Saul. The Jonathan-David cycle begins with several colorful and detailed stories for several reasons: to portray details of Saul's and Jonathan's characters, even before David appears on the scene; to give a sense that Jonathan is a healthy, handsome, successful, and rebellious young man; and to point out that Saul and Jonathan have a father-son relationship in which they are close and dependent upon each other, for, among other reasons, Jonathan is intended to inherit the throne from his increasingly mentally ill father.

The stories that begin the cycle should be read carefully, for they create a situation in which the reader can identify closely with a number of the characters. This background is necessary for a correct understanding of the complicated relationship between Jonathan and David. Of particular importance is Samuel's prophecy at 14:24 and the genealogy at 14:49. But for the purposes of identifying a text of terror, our analysis can begin with 1 Samuel 17. There, all of David's brothers are away serving in Saul's army, so David would occasionally leave the royal palace to go home to Bethlehem to check on his elderly father. One day, while running an errand for his father Jesse, David confronts and slays a frightening Philistine soldier named Goliath. When David the young victor is brought before Saul for his heroism, Saul seems not to recognize this scruffy young hero as being the same nurturing lad whose music had so soothed Saul's torment. But Saul's son Jonathan happens to be present when the conversation takes place, and when Jonathan looks upon David, we are told at that "the soul of Jonathan was knotted to the soul of David, and Jonathan loved him as his own soul." Saul takes David back to the royal palace, forbidding him to leave.

In the palace, the friendship between Jonathan and David grows quickly, and they agree to cement their relationship by making some type of friendship pact, repeatedly referred to in the text as "a covenant," usually with God's name attached to it. We do not know the contents of this covenant, nor do we have a clear model; this is the only time in the Bible that a pact of intimate loyalty is made between same-sex friends. Ordinarily in the Hebrew Bible, a covenant has four characteristics: (1) it is initiated by God, without necessary expectation for a reciprocal human response; (2) a promise is made by God; (3) a tangible sign is given as a continuing reminder of the covenant; and (4) the covenant is articulated as being eternal. The only one of these four marks that is obvious in the "covenant" between Jonathan and David is that it is intended to be eternal.

It should be noted that the pact made between Jonathan and David is mutual; each covenants with the other. Several of the subsequent references in the text make it seem that Jonathan loved David more than David loved Jonathan, but a broader overview of the text would not support that lopsided interpretation. Jonathan is apparently more verbal about his love, but David's actions prove that he loves Jonathan equally. At 18:4 Jonathan, wishing to symbolize his devotion to David, strips off his military princely clothing and, naked, hands it and all his weapons to David.

The gesture is touching and significant. Jonathan's first response to David is to love him, and his second is to make himself vulnerable to him. He strips himself physically, and he hands over to David all his weapons of self-defense. In the process, he discards as well whatever sense of competition may exist between the two men and instead offers David his submission and humility. Jonathan begins as the superior in stature, the privileged prince standing in the company of a scruffy young war hero. But in response to his affection, he discards the symbols of his preferred office and in so doing exalts his friend. Jonathan dramatically risks laying himself open to David, which is a gesture not familiar to contemporary men. The risk is the response of love that enables the friendship to grow and deepen.

At 18:7, when Saul, Jonathan, and David, with all their troops, return from battle with the Philistines, the women of the village come out with timbrels (a version of tambourine) and sing: "Saul has slain his thousands, and David his ten thousands." David, the shepherd boy from Bethlehem who underwent a meteoric rise to acclaim as a military hero, overnight seems to have merited more acclaim than King Saul himself; Jonathan is not even mentioned here. Saul, so mentally ill, is beside himself with rage and is certain that David is conspiring to take the throne away from him. For the first time Saul realizes that this may be he who will fulfill Samuel's prophecy of Saul's downfall.

Saul makes several attempts to kill David. After he fails, Saul decides to neutralize David's growing power and popularity by marrying him into the family. David refuses to marry Saul's oldest daughter Merav, but he does finally agree to marry Saul's youngest daughter Michal, Jonathan's sister. However, as a payment from David in return for giving away his daughter, at 18:25, Saul demands that David bring him one hundred Philistine foreskins. Surely it is Saul's hope that in the process of acquiring the foreskins David will be killed, and the threat to his power will be gone. But David succeeds, thereby acquiring even more power and becoming a great potential threat to the throne of Saul. At 19:1, Saul attempts to convince Jonathan to murder David. Jonathan, of course, refuses to murder his best friend, the man he has so long loved and to whom he has committed himself. The Hebrew text is quite difficult to translate. Though the RSV's "delighted deeply" is an adequate English translation, the more accurate sense of the Hebrew is that David made Jonathan's eyes light up so that Jonathan's heart melted. Jonathan defends David before Saul, and Saul is moved by the plea of his firstborn son, promising at 19:6 to stop his attempts to kill David. Four verses later, the promise is already broken; at 19:10 Saul again attempts to kill David. This time David is protected by Michal. David flees to Samuel for advice, but eventually, at 20:1, he sneaks back for a clandestine meeting with Jonathan.

David pleads with Jonathan to explain why Saul is trying to kill him. At first Jonathan does not believe David; always trusting his father, Jonathan insists that Saul has given his word that he will not try to kill David, since Jonathan has declared his love for David. David insists, and Jonathan begins to grasp some possibility that his father has lied to him. But David pushes the issue further. He is fully aware of Saul's motivations and intentions, but must plot some confrontation that will unmask Saul's deviousness to his own son Jonathan, for Jonathan is still operating under the illusion that he has been taken fully into his father's confidence. At 20:8, David asks Jonathan to find out whether he has actually done something to betray Saul, or whether Saul's mental illness is the source of his anger. David begs Jonathan, on the basis of their deep love for each other (here described as "a Lord's covenant"), that if David has actually done something, Jonathan will himself kill David to protect the family honor. But if it is only Saul's mental illness, David asks Jonathan to help him flee so that he may not lose his life. In this particular passage, we grasp again the depth of their relationship: at 20:3 the odd saying about Jonathan's eyes lighting up so that his heart melts; at 20:4 Jonathan offers to do anything and everything for his friend; at 20:8 they again pledge the depth and permanent loyalty of their commitment to each other; at 20:10 David fears that Saul will abuse Jonathan if he sticks up for David.

At 20:12 the two friends go out into a field, away from the town, there reaffirming their commitment to each other. This mutual commitment is to be eternal, lasting from generation of descendants to generation. Another odd sentence appears in the Hebrew text. These difficult passages almost suggest a pattern: every time the reader seems to get too close to understanding the more intimate details of David and Jonathan's relationship, or the contents of their mysterious "Lord's covenant," the text becomes suddenly unintelligible. The same thing happens at 20:14; the passage is perhaps most accurately translated "While I am still alive, make the faithful love of the Lord with me, that I may not die." We cannot know what this means, but whatever its specifics, it causes the two men to renew their covenant commitment to each other (20:17).

David fails to attend the mandatory ritual meal that regularly celebrates the beginning of the new month because he is so afraid of Saul. Saul hopes to excuse him at first, dreaming up an implausible explanation about David's having had a nocturnal emission, thus being ritually impure. Finally Saul asks Jonathan where David is, and Jonathan mouths the excuse that he and David had manufactured together. In so doing, Jonathan discovers that there is no longer any way he can ingratiate David with Saul again. It may be that Jonathan inadvertently sets off this confrontation; at 20:29, while delivering David's excuse, Jonathan mentions the deep love between him and David. Saul explodes, screaming at Jonathan: "You son of a perverse, rebellious woman, do I not know that you have chosen the son of Jesse to your own shame, and to the shame of your mother's nakedness? So now bring David here that I may kill him with my own hands." Jonathan protests: "Why must you kill David because I love him?" Saul responds by hurling his spear at Jonathan, but misses. Jonathan storms away from the dinner table, grieving because his father has cursed the man to whom Jonathan has committed himself forever and grieving because his mentally ill father has humiliated him.

At 20:35, by prearranged signal, Jonathan lets David know that he will never again be welcomed in Saul's court. The two young men meet again in a field, where they kiss and then collapse in tears into each other's arms, holding each other sobbing until it is difficult to tell which one is more emotionally destroyed. Jonathan leaves David with the words, "Go in peace, for we have sworn ourselves to each other forever. . . . The Lord shall be here in the midst of me and you, and in the midst of my descendants and your descendants, forever." The assumption is that both men, however committed their friendship, will also marry and have children, and that the children will be as bound together as the two men themselves are.

The last time that David and Jonathan see each other is at 23:16. Saul is still pursuing David in order to murder him. Jonathan sneaks out of the palace and travels to meet David at the Wilderness of Zip, in the Negev desert between Jerusalem and the Sinai. There Jonathan comes to his dear friend simply to encourage him in his flight from Saul, to assure David of his love and his confidence that David will eventually become King of Israel and that Jonathan will be his right-hand man and closest personal advisor. The two reaffirm their covenant commitment to each other, the Hebrew says, "before the face of God." But then Jonathan returns home, for though he loves David so deeply, Jonathan has chosen to continue to live at home and to serve as his father Saul's commander-in-chief of the army. He will not let go of his beloved David, nor will he stop seeing him, but at the same time he remains loyal to his father and seeks to assist him in every other way possible.

At the same time that Saul is pursuing David, he is still waging war against the Philistines. In a battle at Mount Gilboa (chapter 31) Jonathan is killed by the Philistines, along with all the rest of his brothers. Saul apparently does not know this, but fearing that he will be captured and tortured to death by the Philistines, he commits suicide—one of the few mentions of suicide in the Bible, which is later contradicted at 2 Sam. 1:10. The Philistines nail the dead bodies of Saul and Jonathan and the other sons to the city walls at Beit Shean, but allies of Saul steal them to give them a proper burial.

In 2 Sam. 1:2, David receives the news of the death of Saul and Jonathan and the ignominious defeat at Mount Gilboa. Having received the news, David has the messenger murdered, and then bursts into one of the most poignant and piercing laments in the Scriptures. The lament cannot fail to bring tears to the eyes of any man who has ever loved another.

> My Jonathan lies shattered on his back in death.
> I ache for you Jonathan, my dear brother,
> you have been so deeply beloved by me,
> and your love for me was so wonderful,
> far surpassing the love of women.

A Text of Terror for Men

This is an extremely complicated story to pick apart because it contains so many themes. But I want to concentrate on why it might be classified as a text of terror for men. Before doing so, however, I must return briefly to the issue of heterosexuality and homosexuality. As I have said, the biblical text is not clear, one way or the other. Rabbinic tradition insists adamantly that their relationship was platonic (*Avot* 5.19). Some American theologians, including a number of bishops, have said they understand this passage as affirming committed male homosexual relationships. But I wonder if Americans are so quick to assume homosexuality here because we have such a limited sense of the broad nonsexual possibilities of passionate same-sex friendship. My own conclusion is that we should ignore the issue of sexual orientation in this story. The Bible, both Old and New Testaments, has no concern one way or the other about committed male homosexual relationships; when either Testament condemns homosexuality, it is referring to male prostitution. I do not believe that the biblical text here focuses on whether Jonathan and David had a sexual relationship or not. Rather, it points to the quality of their friendship and the disaster that can be produced by that kind of beauty.

This leads us to wonder specifically why this text is so terrifying. I suggest four reasons why I believe this to be a text of terror for men. Because the text is so complicated, I am sure others will find nuances I have missed.

First, this is a story about a young man whose father is trying to force him to go into "the family business," although the son does not wish to. The family business, of course, is monarchy. I don't discover in Jonathan any desire to be king. Rather, he keeps throwing the opportunity away through making impetuous moves on the battlefield, through arguing with his father, through stripping off all his symbols of office and handing them to David, through making repeated efforts to save the life of the only person who can overthrow the throne. It is not clear that Jonathan knows what he wants, but the text makes it obvious that he does not wish to follow in his father's footsteps.

Second, this is a story about a son who feels an intense amount of loyalty to an emotionally ill father. Saul's behavior is erratic and irrational. The emotion words used in the text in relationship to Saul are limited to the words "angry, suspicious, afraid," coupled with a number of fierce outbursts in which Saul tries to kill whoever happens to be at hand, including his own heir apparent. But Jonathan never abandons his father; at the beginning of the story, before meeting David, he is Saul's military commander-in-chief. At the end of the story, having said good-bye to David in order to protect him from his father, Jonathan returns home to resume his duties as commander-in-chief, and he ultimately dies on the same battlefield as his father. I do not believe we should call this love, but rather a tragic form of dutiful filial loyalty. One senses that Jonathan does not want to be so absorbed by Saul, but once he has lost David, he does not know how to do anything other than what is expected of him.

Third, this is a story about how suspicious society is of close male friendships. In a class presentation on this story at a local parish some months ago, it was pointed out to me that Saul seems to assume that Jonathan's relationship with David is sexual, even though the story itself never says so overtly. At 20:30, when Saul lashes out at Jonathan during the new-moon dinner, he cries out: "You son of a crooked whore, do you think I can't see that you have chosen the son of Jesse [note he is nameless here, which is a form of dismissal in the biblical text] to your own shame, and to the shame of your mother's nakedness?" Saul's accusation has an obvious sexual content, given the sexual word images of whore, choice, shame, and nakedness, and it seems clear that Saul assumes a sexual relationship between the two young men. Saul is quick to judge, just as our society is quick to judge. When men form close friendships with other men, it is symptomatic of our sexually sick society that so many people are quick to jump to conclusions. Saul chooses the worst possible way to challenge the friendship; he confronts it. Family-systems theories of triangulation point out that a third party can never change the relationship between two other parties by pushing on that relationship. Such pressure only locks the undesired relationship more tightly in place. Saul guarantees Jonathan's love for David and his own exclusion from the relationship with his speech at 20:30.

Fourth, this story makes friendship look dangerous. The men in this story get hurt emotionally, and contemporary men are so unsure about emotions that they avoid them whenever possible, especially the ones that hurt. If we do our job and don't feel very much, we think we are protecting ourselves. Jonathan appears to foul up his career by feeling for David. Since American male identity comes almost exclusively from what we do for a living and whether we succeed at it, the threat of emotions' destroying a career is frightening. Jonathan and David's relationship also seems to set up severe strains at home, which is not unlike the rabbinic idea that friendship outside the family is dangerous to the family. If men make friends at all, it is usually with their wives; same-sex friendships outside of marriage seem to suggest some threat to the husband-wife security. American men know that a level of perfect friendship exists, but we don't know how to get there, and anyway, however much we may desire it, it scares us.

CHAPTER · SIX

Friends, Associates, and Lovers
Jesus, His Male Companions, and the Ancient Ideals of Friendship

Only once in the Bible is a wife ever called a man's friend, at Mal. 2:14. But men learn early that only one type of intimacy is allowed to them—male-female intimacy—and their experience confirms that intimacy necessarily leads to sex. Such identification of cause and effect in one's intimate life brings us back to the prior discussion of heterosexuality and homosexuality. Since intimacy and sex are so linked in male minds, we live in a state of fear that unless we are on guard all the time, we will wind up in bed with our best friend. The easiest way to avoid that upsetting thought is to make sure we never become too intimate friends with another man. But when we fail to love due to fear, we have deprived ourselves of the rewards and the beauty of what both biblical and classical cultures hold as the ultimate ideal of human friendship. How then can we ever learn to value intimacy with another man?

In her novel *Rubyfruit Jungle*, Rita Mae Brown writes of a protagonist, Molly, who has been stunned by the sudden death of her Aunt Jenna. She tries to sneak out of the house for some privacy and air later that night, but observes unexpectedly a scene between her father Carl and her Uncle Ep, who is still mourning his wife's death.

Carrie was asleep so I crawled out of bed and crept down the hall covered with peeling green wallpaper with white gardenias on it. I was planning to hotfoot it out on the porch and watch the stars but I never made it because Ep and Carl were in the living room and Carl was holding Ep. He had both arms around him and every now and then he'd smooth down Ep's hair or put his cheek next to his head. Ep was crying just like Leroy. I couldn't make out what they were saying to each other. A couple times I could hear Carl telling Ep he had to hang on, that's all anybody can do is hang on. I was afraid they were going to get up and see me so I hurried back to my room. I've never seen men hold each other. I thought the only things they were allowed to do was shake hands or fight. But if Carl was holding Ep maybe it wasn't against the rules. Since I wasn't sure, I thought I'd keep it to myself and never tell. I was glad they could touch each other. Maybe all men did that after everyone went to bed so no one would know the toughness was for show. Or maybe they only did it when someone died. I wasn't sure at all and it bothered me.

Do men in contemporary America touch each other only clandestinely, "so no one would know the toughness was for show"? Is there any sense of intimacy left between men in our society? Does the term "friendship" have meaning for us any longer?

Traditions of Male Friendship

In Book Eight of his *Nicomachean Ethics*, Aristotle discusses the male motivation to friendship: to be friends, men must (*a*) feel goodwill toward each other, (*b*) be aware of each other's goodwill, and (*c*) each possess qualities that are lovable to the other. He then goes on to identify three types or classes of male-male friendship, each of which presumes the above three qualifications, but each of which exists in order to satisfy a different purpose. The first type Aristotle calls friendship of utility. Here two men care enough for each other to assist each other. This friendship may take the form of helping each other with business problems (as long as it does not violate some sense of competitiveness between them), car-pooling, authoring a project together, or giving advice, though this is not to be confused with a mentoring situation or a teacher-student relationship. As Aristotle points out, such relationships do not necessarily carry any sense of love for the other, for ultimately the investment in the relationship is self-serving and seeks personal benefit under the guise of friendship. When there is nothing to be gained, no favor to be done, no mutual goal to be achieved, such friends spend less time together, and thus the two friends drift apart when the benefits begin to decrease. No matter how pleasurable the relationship, if it is ultimately structured so that each party is most interested in getting his own needs met, it is the lowest of Aristotle's three forms of friendship.

The second type of friendship Aristotle discusses is friendship of pleasure. This too has a strong self-serving element, for as he points out, "we enjoy the society of witty people not because of what they are in themselves, but because they are agreeable to us." These friendships have more emotion in them than the utilitarian type, though they are prone to a certain fragility or transience as our emotional needs or our tastes and preferences change. Even this type is somewhat unusual for adult men; it is more typical of young men who simply "hang out" together and enjoy each other's company so much that they do not need an external project or self-serving goal to justify spending time together. A friend told me once of calling his father from whom he had been estranged since his parents divorced several years earlier. He asked to spend some vacation time with his father, who was aging, so that they could know each other as adults. His father's response was to offer to concoct a project that they could do together. For many adult men the idea of simply being together to experience the pure pleasure of each other's company, without any additional socially acceptable justification, is frightening. It is particularly so when it means two men relaxing together in a room for an extended period of time without the company of women.

The third type of friendship Aristotle discusses is perfect friendship. This is the highest form, the least common, and the one that most resembles the relationship between Jonathan and David. Aristotle understands that such a relationship involves a commitment to a mutually held set of values and a willingness to be emotionally intimate with each other. Such a friendship cannot exist unless the two men complement each other and have healthy mature characters. Each wishes the good of the other above his own personal good. Each is in service to the other without desire for reciprocity. Each enjoys the pleasure of the other innocently and absolutely. Each is healthy enough to recognize the good in the other because he recognizes the good in himself. Such a relationship is the perfect form of community between two men and is characterized by sayings such as "Friends have one soul between them," or "A friend is another self" [alter ego].

At the heart of such perfect friendship lies an intimacy foreign to most American males; hence we see the frequency with which Jonathan and David are held suspect of homosexual involvement. Intimate friendship is by its nature erotic, as Plato understood. In his *Symposium*, he speaks in the voice of Socrates in order to construct a philosophy of Eros, a powerful spirit born of the seduction of the drunken god Resource (the son of Cunning) by the goddess Poverty. But while born from a somewhat suspect pairing, Eros is also born on the birthing day of Aphrodite, and hence Eros and Aphrodite are linked forever by their shared moment of origin. For Socrates, Eros is that which desires union with the beautiful, the wise, the good, in order to "father," through "impregnation" of another person, the ultimate values of prudence and virtue. But of interest in the reading of Plato's *Symposium* is that he seems to understand such "impregnation" as happening between two intimately intertwined people, regardless of their gender. In other words, Eros is just as much an integral part of the relationship between two deeply committed men as it is between a man and a woman, for true Eros transcends, though may also include, the carnal. It is this intensity, this yearning for union, between two close male friends that is so frightening to many males.

One may take the argument a step further by asserting that the matter of physical contact between two intimate friends is of little concern to the Greek philosophers. Upper- and upper-middle-class Greek males often formed a kind of "companionship club" devoted to the intimate exchange of profound ideas that would foster prudence and virtue. In such voluntary communities, one sought-after value was consubstantiality, that is, the merging of two people into one body, so that their two faces formed the illusion of one face (see Gabriel Herman, *Ritualised Friendship and the Greek City*; compare also with the term *yehidut* in the Hassidic tradition). Within these communities feasting rituals and hospitality rituals were extremely important, and at times they even merged. Two who shared a meal, or sat at the same table, were assumed to share a common substance, creating a bond the violation of which was deemed more heinous than homicide.

To some degree, a modified form of this bonding affected the later Christian valuation of breaking bread together, of *com-pagne* (with bread), of creating a "company" that was the purest embodiment of community. What apparently did not enter Christian eucharistic tradition was the recognition, within the Greek male companionship clubs, that intense personal relationships sometimes needed to be expressed as mutual carnal pleasure. Such occasional sharing of physical pleasure between two intimate male friends (*hetairoi*), or on occasion between a man and a woman who could participate in the generally male clubs, was cause for neither concern nor prurient interest. It was simply recognized that close friendship of Aristotle's third type had an inherent erotic character that was not the dominant characteristic of the friendship, but occasionally spilled over into a need for expression.

Here then we discover yet a further nuancing to Zeno's maxim "A friend is an alternative self" (Diogenes Laertius, *Lives of the Eminent Philosophers*, VII:23). True friendship assumes a level of intimacy that is its primary value, although it may include the consequent value of an erotic desire for union of the self to another. The third level of Aristotelian friendship, shared values and complementary intimacy, is impossible to American males as long as they fear intimacy with other males. It may help to understand that erotic feelings are a natural part of deep same-sex friendship, and while they are normal, it is not necessary that they be acted upon genitally.

The fear that American men have of such friendships is ultimately not a fear of others, but a fear of themselves—a fear that they will be overcome by their own unexpected homoerotic urge and then "act the woman." Ralph Waldo Emerson tells the following story: "On the Alps, the traveller sometimes beholds his own shadow magnified to a giant, so that every gesture of his hand is terrific. 'My children,' said an old man to his boys scared by a figure in the dark entry, 'my children, you will never see anything worse than yourselves.' " A critical part of what makes us fear friendship is not that we cannot control others, but fear that we cannot control ourselves. We are faced with the task of learning to savor our emotions and urges in the awareness that mature men can make mature decisions about their own human responses. If ultimately we control our biological responses to women, why does it so frighten us that we might not control similar responses to men?

Essays spelling out the character and philosophy of friendship are common in the classical Greek period. Plutarch's "Erotic Essay" on his love for a friend is deeply touching, and there are many similar essays throughout the broad literature of the period. We find paeans to friendship in Jewish tradition beginning with medieval period writers such as Leo Habraeus, Yehiel of Pisa. While rabbinic tradition generally ignores the relationship between Jonathan and David, the Talmud does speak often of friendship, and much is made of the "exclusive" friendship of David and Ahitophel in both Pirkei Avot and Kallah Rabbati VIII. In early Christian tradition, friendship appears to take on an emphasis designed to neutralize the intensity of intimacy in same-sex friendship, perhaps in order to protect the nuclear family.

Essays on the value of same-sex friendship are not limited to the classical, rabbinic, or patristic traditions. Among the greatest contemporary examples continuing the tradition are two essays by the nineteenth-century American writer Ralph Waldo Emerson: "On Self-Reliance" and "On Friendship." They read as though Emerson had David and Jonathan in mind as he wrote. He argues that true friendship, which we have already designated as Aristotle's third type, is based on two essential qualities: truth and tenderness. Truth is a rare commodity within our deceitful society and demands an extraordinary courage. "A friend is a person with whom I may be sincere. . . . But to most of us society shows not its face and eye, but its side and its back. To stand in true relations with men in a false age is worth a fit of insanity, is it not?" Those with courage must also be tender in order to become intimate friends. Deriding much of the silliness of what we now call male bonding (he scorns it as "silken and perfumed amity"), Emerson goes on to define what a tender friendship looks like:

> The end of friendship is a commerce the most strict and homely that can be joined. . . . It is for aid and comfort through all the relations

and passages of life and death. It is fit for serene days, and graceful gifts, and country rambles, but also for rough roads and hard fare, shipwreck, poverty, and persecution. It keeps company with the sallies of the wit and the trances of religion. We are to dignify to each other the daily needs and offices of man's life, and embellish it by courage, wisdom, and unity. It should never fall into something usual and settled, but should be alert and inventive, and add rhyme and reason to what was drudgery.

Though not named, Emerson insists that a third quality is also essential to true friendship, echoing the classical philosophers: that a friend be an alter ego. Complementarity is an artful combination of likeness and unlikeness, in which the strength of character of each person is blatant and unmistakable. Such friendships even thrive on rough treatment of each other, assuming that the love upon which they are based is never called into doubt. Emerson writes: "I hate, where I looked for a manly furtherance, or at least a manly resistance, to find a mush of concession. The only joy I have in his being mine, is that the *not mine* is *mine*. . . . Better be a nettle in the side of your friend than his echo." Each is who he is, simultaneously completely different and yet like the other. One's own thoughts sound new and larger in the mouth of the other; yet one is to the other a beautiful enemy, untamable, and devoutly revered.

There can never be deep peace between two spirits, never mutual respect, until, in their dialogue, each stands for the whole world. What is so great as friendship, let us carry with what grandeur of spirit we can. Let us be silent—so we may hear the whisper of the gods. . . . The only reward of virtue is virtue; the only way to have a friend is to be one. . . . In the last analysis, love is only the reflection of a man's own worthiness from other men. Men have sometimes exchanged names with their friends, as if they would signify that in their friend each loved his own soul.

Intimate same-sex friendships, like that of Jonathan and David, are the training ground for a love that is not inhibited by fears of gender or of the limitations of commitment, but a love that seeks virtue and wisdom everywhere. Friendship is the primary channel of both virtue and wisdom by which the social world of humanity is redeemed. Such intimate friendships are the reflection of God's *hesed*, God's unshakably committed fidelity, to creation. We Christians have come to recognize in such friendships an imitation of the love of Christ toward those who recognize him.

Jesus and His Companions

Written records suggest two things of special interest about Jesus: he may have used the term "friend" more often than did his rabbinic contemporaries, and typical to his times, he was much more often found in the company of men than of women. Because Christianity has so long cherished the value of our imitating Christ in his manner of life and thinking, it is important to explore the New Testament models of the way Jesus interacted with those men who were among his close circle of followers. If the age-old claim is true that the *imitatio Christi* is one expression of God's will for humanity, then surely it must touch upon that important arena of human relationship, friendship. What did Jesus teach concerning friendship? What was the quality of those friendships he enjoyed?

To understand the friendship teachings of Jesus, one is tempted to seek a distinction among the pertinent Greek terms *hetairos*, *philos*, and *mathētēs* and to try to connect each to Hebrew or Aramaic equivalents, such as *haver*, *yedid*, or *ohev*. Any connection is conjecture, for the sources do not bear out exact definition, yet it might be productive to toy with these equations:

$$hetairos \ = \ yedid$$
$$philos \ = \ haver$$
$$math\bar{e}t\bar{e}s \ = \ ohev$$

The Hebrew word *yedid* is common in the Hebrew Bible (e.g. Deut. 33:12; Isa. 5:1; 2 Sam. 12:25) and in rabbinic literature. But in the Gospels we find its conjectured Greek equivalent, *hetairos*, only in Matthew, and there in contradictory manners. *Hetairos* is used twice in parables as a form of address to distant comrades (Matt. 20:13 and 22:12), once to refer to Judas at the betrayal in Gethsemane (26:50), and once (in a variant textual reading) as an address by children to each other (Matt. 11:16). Thus we cannot make a direct comparison

98

to *yedid*, which means an unusually close friend. *Hetairos* does not appear in the other three Gospel accounts. Nor can the Gospel's use of *hetairos* be compared to its general use in Greek and Roman philosophical literature, as *hetairos* was explained previously in relation to companionship clubs: close intimate friends, often of the same sex, who are of the same economic class and intellectual background, and who hold the same set of elevated values.

Philos is the most common Greek word for friend in the Gospels, just as the Hebrew word *haver* is in the rabbinic literature. Yet even *philos* does not appear consistently throughout the Gospels. We find it once in Matt. 11:19 (an "associate" of publicans and sinners), not at all in Mark, six times in John, and fourteen times in Luke.

The meaning of *philos* is not consistent throughout the Gospel of John. At 3:29 and 15:14-15, it has the same sense as "brother" in the Babylonian Talmud, tractate Sota 40:a: "If you listen to me, you are my brothers; if you do not, you are my people, and I shall rule you tyrannically." Assuming that these two works mean the same thing by the word *brother*, we understand that those who listen to the words of Jesus are his friends, while those who do not listen still remain his people to whom he will be loyal but benevolently dictatorial. The sense of *philos* in these two Johannine passages, perhaps like that of *haver*, seems to be one of commitment without a necessary intimacy. Yet *philos* is also used to describe both Jesus' relationship to Lazarus (John 11:11) and Pilate's relationship to Caesar (John 19:12), two usages which seem irreconcilable, since one connotes intimacy and the other connotes political authority.

Jesus' famous phrase in John 15:15, "I no longer call you slaves . . . but I have called you friends [*philoi*]," employs the Greek plural form *philoi* without a clear sense of specific definition other than that it means something quite different from "servant." Some light might be shed on the John 15 use of the friend/slave paradigm by comparing it with a line from the traditional Jewish prayer *Ha Yom Harat Olam*: "This day the world was called into being; this day all the creatures of the universe stand in judgment before You as children (*banim*) or as slaves (*avadim*). If as children, have pity on us as a father pities his children; if as slaves, we call upon You to be gracious unto us and merciful in judgment." The intention of John 15, then, is to emphasize the intimacy of relationship between Jesus and his followers as an intimacy typical to blood relatives, as opposed to the distance more typical of a master-slave relationship. The commitment that a parent feels toward a child is different from the commitment that an employer feels toward an employee. In this instance, *philoi* means those with whom we have a relationship similar to blood-intimacy, but without suggesting a sense of friendship as we understand it in the twentieth century.

The meaning of "friends" in Jesus' other famous phrase, "Greater love hath no one than this, that one lay down one's life for one's *philoi*" (John 15:13), is equally vague. In context it carries a sense more akin to the Hebrew term *re'a*, or neighbor, than to close intimate association (see *re'a* in this sense of neighbor, for example, at Ps. 88:18, where a friend and a neighbor are two distinct categories). The expectation seems to be that a follower of Jesus should be willing to make the ultimate sacrifice for anyone to whom he or she is committed, even if only by physical proximity, whether that commitment includes intimate bonding or not.

The use of *philos* in Luke is equally irregular in meaning. Most often it carries the same sense as the Hebrew word *haver*, "associate" (see Luke 7:6, 7:34, 11:5, 11:6, 11:8, 12:4, 14:10, 14:12, 15:6, 15:9, 15:29). Among those counted as associates (*philoi*) in these passages seem to include army buddies, dinner guests, neighbors, drop-in visitors from out-of-town, business colleagues, and adolescent friends. At Luke 16:9, one of the "difficult sayings," Jesus counsels his followers to become *philoi* of the mammon of unrighteousness, but surely he does not suggest a merging of deeply held values. At Luke 23:12, in a sense similar to John 19:12, Pilate and Herod are described as *philoi* of each other. At Luke 21:16, *philoi* are among the list of those to be feared, for they will turn the followers of Jesus over to the authorities for persecution and death.

The Gospel of John also contains the mysterious figure referred to as "the beloved disciple." The Greek word *mathētēs* means nothing more than "disciple," and thus could apply to any of the Twelve, or even to the millions of Christians who have come after. Comparison of the Septuagint and Hebrew texts suggests that the normal parallel for the Greek *mathētēs* is the Hebrew *talmid*, meaning student, disciple, learner. Yet the possibility remains that the original Hebrew or Aramaic word behind the Gospel use here of *mathētēs* is instead another Hebrew synonym for *haver* and *yedid*—the word *ohev*. *Ohev* in this particular sense is used at Prov. 18:24—"There are companions to keep one company, but there is an *ohev* who cleaves tighter than a brother"—and is derived from the Hebrew word root *AHV*, meaning "love." Thus an *ohev* may be a friend who has with him the sense of lover, here approaching Aristotle's third type of friendship, that of intimacy and commitment to mutual values. We find the beloved disciple acting in close physical intimacy with Jesus (13:23-25 and 21:20); adopting Jesus' mother after the crucifixion (19:26-27); recognizing the risen Christ when others do not (21:7); and attaining a mythical status among the company of primitive Christians (21:20-24) as the one so intimate with Jesus that he would be the initial witness to the second coming.

But even with all this information, we cannot deduce from word study what patterns of male friendship were natural to Jesus, beyond the suggestion that with at least one of his disciples he had a friendship of unusual physical and emotional intimacy. The Greek words are used too inconsistently to give us adequate information, and they do not correlate specifically or clearly enough with the assumed Hebrew or Aramaic antecedents. Jesus may have used the word "friend" more often than his rabbinic contemporaries, or perhaps it is simply that the Gospel writers are more influenced by Hellenistic expectations and so portrayed a Semitic Jesus speaking thoughts typical to a non-Semitic culture.

We certainly know that Hellenistic philosophy's interest in patterns and values of friendship continued long after Aristotle and well past the time of the writing of the New Testament. In his Epistle 6, the Latin philosopher Seneca (ca. 4 B.C.E.–65 C.E.) wrote to his male friend concerning their relationship:

> I therefore wish to impart to you this sudden change in myself: I should then begin to place a surer trust in our friendship—the true friendship, which hope and fear and self-interest cannot sever, the friendship in which and for the sake of which men meet death. I can show you many

who have lacked, not a friend, but a friendship; this, however, cannot possibly happen when souls are drawn together by identical inclinations into an alliance of honourable desires. And why can it not happen? Because in such cases men know that they have all things in common, especially their troubles.

A century later, Seneca's successor Hierocles also wrote on "Fraternal Love," characterizing the Aristotelian third type of friendship (the alter ego) as one between "brothers." In a passage reminiscent of St. Paul's metaphor in 1 Corinthians 12 of the church as the body of Christ, Hierocles writes (*On Duties* 4.17.20):

> The first bit of advice, therefore, is very clear, easily obtained, and common to all people. For it is a sound word which everyone will recognize as clear: Treat anybody whatsoever as though you supposed that he were you and you he. . . . The precept is singularly adapted to the common topic of brothers, since the man who is considering how to treat his brother need begin with no other presupposition than promptly to assume their natural sameness. . . . In the next place, we should consider that in a certain way a person's brothers are parts of him, just as my eyes are of me, and similarly my hands, and the rest. . . . If the eyes and hands, therefore, should each receive its own soul and mind, they would treat the rest with respect in every way possible on account of the partnership we have mentioned before, because they would not be able to perform their own functions without the presence of the other members. In the same way also, we who are men and admit to having a soul should in no way relax the esteem with which we should deal with our brothers. Furthermore, brothers far more than parts of the body are adapted by nature to help each other. For the eyes, indeed, being present with each other, see together, and one hand works together with the other that is present. But the cooperation of brothers with each other is much more varied, for they do things which by common consent are excellent even if they should be completely separated from each other, and they greatly benefit each other even if the distance that separates them is immense. (trans. Malherbe)

Historically, Christian friendship was ultimately to be a sterilized, spiritualized form of Hellenism that superseded both the rabbinic heritage typical to Jesus as well as the more embodied intimacy of Greek and Roman intellectual debating societies.

Jesus' patterns of male friendship will perhaps become more apparent through the study of the Gospel records of his behavior. Did Jesus call his disciples "friends"? Was Lazarus, who was not among the Twelve, a closer friend than Peter, who was? Were Jesus and John the Baptist friends? Did the apostles' teamwork with Jesus lead to friendship, and if so, which of Aristotle's three types of friendship might best characterize the relationship?

The Gospels preserve a general picture of Jesus as a storyteller, a teacher, and a companion to others in the quest for spiritual rectitude. The Gospels do not portray Jesus as necessarily warm and accessible, nor as unusually extroverted. Although he healed, he made such gestures of concern reluctantly on occasion. He often shunned crowds (in Mark 7:24 he even flees to Lebanon!) and at times seemed to fear them. We are repeatedly told of his lack of concern for the nuclear family (Matt. 10:35, 12:48, 19:29, and parallels), and we are not sure whether he had a committed marital relationship or children of his own. He had preferential friendships and more often sought out the company of Peter and Lazarus, Andrew and Philip, Mary and Martha, and the Magdalene, than the company of others. This affirmed that his peers were more important to him than his parents and siblings. Many of the feelings that we normally associate with loyalty to family seem to have been transferred by Jesus onto his relationship with God. The Gospels do not speak of his father Joseph during Jesus' adult ministry, yet the Gospel of John (almost exclusively among the four Gospels) portrays Jesus as preferring to call God "father" more often than the various other names and titles by which God could also be invoked. In this Jesus is not unique, for both Greek and rabbinic literatures record that Jesus' contemporaries also frequently called God "father." These same rabbinic contemporaries often referred to the particularly pious among them as "sons of God" (the claim is not blasphemous; see Luke 3:30, in which Adam is called the son of God).

The "Feminine" Values of Jesus

Though we know remarkably little of Jesus' personality, we have a hint that he questioned the public perception of his own masculine identity. At Matt. 16:13, he turns to his frequent companions in order to ask a question that men today ask of each other: "What sort of man do you perceive me to be?" Underneath the layers of later Christian messianic interpretation lies a question of male identity: "Will you tell me who you understand me to be?" Peter answers that he sees Jesus as someone in whom God is intimately at work. At this moment of crisis in his ministry, Jesus turns to the community of men for affirmation of his masculine identity. Such a question is rare even today, for it assumes a level of trust and vulnerability between men that many cannot yet achieve.

Why did such a powerful identity as Jesus' need affirmation from others? Perhaps because the values that Jesus taught were what we would now call "feminine" values: humility, mercy, suffering, patience, fidelity, submission, sharing, purity, equality, cooperation, reconciliation, and pacifism. He taught his disciples to spread his values, but not to worry about success or predictable results (Matt. 10:5-28). Traditional American male values, insofar as they promote success and predictable results, are often categorically opposed to the values of Jesus. In fact, the values that Jesus condemned are exactly those usually rewarded in the male business world, the military-industrial complex, the political arena, and even the institutional church. At John 6:15, Jesus specifically rejects temporal success and power, and at Matt. 12:8 Jesus asserts that the needs of individual humans must always take precedence over the needs of institutions, even the need for success.

In Matt. 15:19, Jesus says that it is not what goes into a person's mouth that defiles, but that which comes out of a person's mouth. The quotation and its contemporary applications continue to challenge us: "the things which defile a man are evil thoughts [scheming how to use others for personal advancement], murders [gossip and rumors], adulteries [disloyalty to commitments], fornications [the abuse of women, in so many ways], thefts [dishonest business dealings], false witness [not telling the truth to other men], blasphemies [self-reliance, rugged independence]." An even longer and more condemning list can be found at Mark 7:21-22.

At Mark 10:35, Jesus rejects the very foundation of our society's corporate and ecclesiastical power-mongering, the old-boy network.

FRIENDS, ASSOCIATES, AND LOVERS

According to the story, two of the Twelve, brothers James and John, come to Jesus and request that he use his "insider" authority to assure them a place of privilege in the coming kingdom. Jesus sternly refuses their request and instructs them that favoritism and power-mongering have no place in a society that is pleasing to God. In the coming kingdom, the cardinal virtues will include humility and the equality of all. Interestingly, when the same story is told at Luke 22:24 no disciples are mentioned by name, and in Matt. 20:20, the two are protected by shifting the blame to their mother. We hear a continuing condemnation of our contemporary corporate and ecclesiastical structures at Luke 14:13-14. There Jesus insists that the rewards of the resurrection will be available solely to those who have consciously and publicly contradicted the chauvinist structures of authority, which promote supporters of the status quo.

Jesus was not afraid of male touch; in fact he employed it even beyond the purposes of physical healing. As we have already seen, he held the beloved disciple. But at Matt. 17:1-7, when the disciples are afraid at the transfiguration, Jesus comforts them by touching them. At Matt. 19:13-14 he beckons the weak and vulnerable to draw near to his physical person. He washes the feet of his followers at John 13—an act as erotic as it is humbling. Jesus refers to himself as a nurturer at Luke 13:34 (a mother hen who shelters her chicks) and again at John 16:21 (a woman who is in the birth pangs of labor).

According to the Gospel records, and to Matthew 9–12 in particular, Jesus spent most of his time within the community of men. The members of this community were markedly diverse; what held them together was their commitment, not their homogeneity or their similar stages of personal and spiritual development. His time among them was focused and intimate; when he was with men, they held a place of honor in his eyes. He was capable of forming close friendships with men and seems to have spent more time with them than with women. He appears to have modeled a style of male-male friendship that was committed, intimate, honest, open, and even dependent. Even in the Garden of Gethsemane, his most vulnerable moment of trial, he begged his disciples to stay awake and be strong for him. Comfortably and seemingly without role conflict, Jesus could be simultaneously leader, teacher, and intimate friend of his male followers.

But there is no record that Jesus and his male followers did "men's things" together. They did not go hunting together, as do contemporary men, nor did they share off-color jokes. They did not compete with each other (aside from James' and John's requests at Mark 10:35), nor did they tell each other lies in order to make themselves look good in each other's company (see Matt. 16:21-23). The power and influence of Jesus in the lives of his followers arose from the depth of their committed mutual relationship and from the love, honesty, and dignity they showed to each other.

Ultimately we do not have a solid enough outline in Jesus' teachings to articulate a comprehensive philosophy of Christian friendship. The role of friendship in the church has been as much a product of nonbiblical influences as of New Testament teachings. There are two aspects of Jesus' behavior, however, that provide particular hope for men who are changing. The first is the values exhibited in Jesus' life: compassion, integrity, flexibility, humility, mercy, pacifism, patience, fidelity, generosity, cooperativeness, intellectual honesty, and dependence on the community of men. Even if his relationship with the disciples was only utilitarian rather than Aristotle's third type of intimacy, as the record would suggest, he volunteered to lay down his life for his *philoi*, and challenged them to follow his example.

The second note of hope is Jesus' bravery in the face of a newness within God's continually unfolding revelation. Change is difficult, and Jesus recognized this in his teachings. At Matt. 12:43-45, he spoke of our temptation to return to the familiar comfort of what we once knew rather than face the creative insecurity of differentness:

> When the unclean spirit has gone out of a person, it wanders through waterless regions looking for a resting place, but it finds none. Then it says, "I will return to my house from which I came." When it is come, it finds it empty, swept, and put in order. Then it goes and brings along seven other spirits more evil than itself, and they enter in and live there: and the last state of that person is worse than the first.

Once we have begun to change, we are called to keep our eyes set on the new creation and not to look back. Christians can recognize the new Adam in Jesus insofar as he was willing to cherish his own human nature, in all its vulnerability, and yet to turn his face bravely toward an unknown future in which he and the world that he knew would be very different.

PART · TWO

Prayer, Iron John, and the White Snake

CHAPTER · SEVEN

Masculine Stumbling Blocks to Prayer

A ny discussion of masculine spirituality must begin with agreed-upon definitions of the terms "spirituality" and "masculine," in order to be able to build upon a common foundation. The contemporary men's movement is led primarily by Christians and Jews, however loosely they may define themselves, and also has an unusual sensitivity to Native American spirituality. In order to be inclusive, spirituality must be defined so that it makes room for the broad spectrum of men who are addressing change. A useful definition of spirituality, then, is as follows: the human desire or urge to establish a relationship with that Power or Being that transcends our human limitations, including our gender-specific limitations, without invalidating or destroying those limitations.

We all have the urge to invest ourselves in something beyond our immediate finitude. For men, this investment takes different forms: dedication to career and financial security; power in the corporate or political realm; athletic prowess; a relationship with spouse or lover or children; wisdom and superior intellectual knowledge. For others, the investment takes the shape of being the most notorious drunk or womanizer, manipulator or "bad boy" in the neighborhood, for after all, according to Alfred Adler, to succeed at one of these is also a form of achievement and power.

PRAYER, IRON JOHN, AND THE WHITE SNAKE

For some, the investment in the transcendent takes the form of a quest for God or something like God, a Power or a Being that breaks the confines of human limitation, allowing us as men to know we are not alone in this universe in spite of our role stereotype of self-sufficiency. Nor will that which we have built simply vanish at our deaths. It is this quest for the transcendent, this investment in a Power or Being larger than ourselves, that I mean when I say "spiritual." It is perhaps best to leave the definition this vague, for as we fear religious pluralism less and less, we men are discovering commonalities between us in our spiritual quests that need no longer be entrapped in the more technical or exclusive language of specific religious truth-claims. However, many of my own observations that follow draw specifically on the Christian tradition, since that is the tradition with which I am most familiar.

The word "masculine" is even harder to define due to the accretions to the word of many cultural stereotypes and assumptions. I do not mean "masculine" in the way it has often been used, such as a synonym for virile or manly or particularly as an integral part of the vocabulary of homophobia. If, for example, one smells the colognes marketed as masculine scents, one finds a wide variety of different scents, all of which seem, in at least someone's opinion, to be appropriate for men to wear. Whereas men used to wear only Witch Hazel, Old Spice, or English Leather, they are now encouraged to wear scents that are softer, sweeter, and more flowery. Recently, in fact, a cosmetic company admitted that it uses exactly the same formula to scent its men's products as its women's products; it merely changes the labels to call one feminine and one masculine. As further examples, who would dare any longer to claim that cooking is not masculine or that nurturing our own children is not masculine? In both cases, it was only a few decades ago when these tasks were considered to be unfit for "real men."

Because the definition of masculine has become so unclear in our culture, it is best here to limit our use of the term "masculine" in the phrase "masculine spirituality" to the following: that which is appropriate to those males who have taken seriously the opportunity for their own liberation from gender stereotypes and have in the process begun to seek a new and more sensitive self-understanding in light of the feminist critique. James Nelson calls men who fit this definition "recovering sexists." Through such a careful definition, the term "masculine" still belongs to males, but it is removed from cultural associations with virility, violence, emotional distancing, and the abuse of power. These sorts of cultural assumptions function simply as troublesome barriers to the free expression and exploration of male identity.

Having delineated what is meant by the term "masculine spirituality," we must next identify twelve specific stumbling blocks that inhibit the development of a healthy contemporary masculine spirituality within the Christian tradition:

1. The identification in the tradition of God as Father.
2. The fear of the feminine.
3. The domination by tradition-centered males of the development of almost all literature in theology and spiritual direction.
4. The suppression by males of much of the broad range of human emotions.
5. The valuation of self-sufficiency, making it hard to pray for help or to seek healing in the face of powerlessness.
6. The misunderstanding of the value and process of reciprocal relationships, which inhibits our sense of self in God's eyes and devalues our interdependence with creation and with the rest of humanity.
7. The insistence that to *do* something is categorically more manly than to *be* something, or simply *to be*.
8. The problem men have knowing who they are when they are not in charge.
9. The heritage of body-soul dualism and the concomitant dismissal of the body and human sexuality.
10. The need to control structurelessness by putting everything in a hierarchical order; the fear of both chaos and spontaneity.
11. The assumption that incompleteness or unpredictable result is a sign of failure.
12. The preference for linearity over circularity, particularly as conditioned by male anatomy and phallocentrism.

PRAYER, IRON JOHN, AND THE WHITE SNAKE

The Tradition of God as "Father"

In his seminal book *Finding Our Fathers*, Harvard psychologist Samuel Osherson explores the troubled relationships that adult men have with their fathers, whether still living or not, and particularly the situation of adult men caught between living fathers and living sons. I have never met a father who set out to be a parenting failure, as he may be perceived by his son; nonetheless, many men carry negative memories of their fathers. They remember them as judgmental, emotionally or physically cold and inaccessible, and frighteningly powerful with explosive moods. Some fathers are remembered as being so difficult to please that men struggle long into adulthood to prove themselves worthy of love. Perhaps this is why we are so surprised at the incredible forgiveness of the father figure in the story of the prodigal son (Luke 15). We seem not to expect fathers to forgive so unconditionally, although we might expect it of mothers. Of course, not all men have powerful memories of rejection and distancing from their fathers, but the literature of the men's movement indicates that it is by far the majority experience of men presently in their thirties and older.

When we speak of God exclusively as father, we human beings tend to project upon God the same set of characteristics that we remember from our own earthly fathers, or perhaps we choose to project some inverse set of characteristics as compensation or apology. In either case, God is not free to be God, nor are we men free to appreciate the softer, more accessible, more unconditionally forgiving aspects of God's love. In the extreme, God and father get all mixed up so that some men carry around an image of "the wounded God" that is no different from "the wounded father" of their own childhood. (The term "wounded father" offers a way of understanding the dysfunction our fathers passed on to us, without blaming them; they too were victims of a twisted heritage of expectations and limitations.) The literature in the field of men's studies suggests that some men need to be encouraged symbolically to "kill" the memories of their bad father in order to let the truly good father emerge. After symbolically or ritually resolving the misunderstandings buried within childhood memories, these men can intentionally seek new forms and methods of communication between an adult son and aging father. While this therapeutic work may be a necessity within father-son relationships, "killing the wounded God" is not necessarily a positive concept in the spiritual life of men. The stumbling block could easily be avoided by opening up possibilities of addressing God in terms other than father. The practice of addressing the deity in feminine terms or in nonparental terms is well attested in both Scripture and tradition. As Christians we must understand that when Jesus taught us to call God Abba, he offered that as a possible, but not as the only allowable, form of address. It was not a form intended to exclude the many other theological understandings of God.

Fear of the Feminine

It may be that men do not easily switch to calling God "mother" for reasons that have nothing to do with Scripture and the received tradition. For example, many men might be uncomfortable understanding themselves as created in the image of the mother God because they have been taught from their childhood to avoid anything that smacks of a feminine self-identification. Perhaps that is why so many of the scriptural references to God as feminine have been suppressed in our usual English translations. For example, the Hebrew text of Hos. 11:9 reads: "I will not destroy Ephraim, for I am [the God] El, but *I am not a male*; therefore I will not come forth in a violent rage." Most standard English texts do not make this nonmale image of God evident at all. Similarly, intimacy with the human Jesus (as opposed to the disembodied Christ) may carry a taint of homosexuality for some men, in spite of the medieval monastic tradition of writing sexually explicit poetry about Jesus as one's male lover (see for example the poetry of Jacopone da Todi). In a similar obsession with the maleness of Christ, one of the early church controversies was whether women at their resurrection might have penises restored to them, in order that they be truly whole (see for example, Augustine, *The City of God*, xxii.17).

Many men have been taught to shun whatever smacks of "playing the woman's role," for they do not know how to define masculinity other than by a sequence of "nots": not feminine, not womanly, not passive-receptive, not soft, not "on bottom." For such men, the assumed maleness of God functions as a secure refuge from any hint of age-old accusation that religious faith is for women, the elderly, and the weak. The assumed maleness of God then confirms that all within the human *imago* that is not male is somehow suspicious and that only human males are safe in knowing that they bear the stamp of God's likeness. Indeed when the early church fathers spoke about women, they often agreed with Augustine (*De Trinitatie*, XII.7.10), who claimed that only males are made in the image of God and that females get the opportunity to share that image a little only by marrying a man, but never in their own right.

Male-dominated Theology and Spirituality

Of the various books of the Hebrew Bible and the New Testament, scholars conjecture that only two may have been written by women: the Book of J and the Revelation of St. John the Divine. Elisabeth Schüssler Fiorenza has convincingly pointed out that the memory of women is effectively suppressed within the primitive church and its writings, although we know that the reputation of earliest diaspora Christianity was as a religion that appealed primarily to women, the elderly, and the marginalized. Among the vast heritage of postbiblical theological literature, there is next to no acknowledged authorship by women, though it should be noted that the Sayings of the Desert Fathers frequently include the words of St. Syncletice, so should in reality be called the Sayings of the Desert Fathers and Mothers. The history of the literature of Christian spirituality contains a few more names of women, though they are precious few; some have recently come to our attention again, such as Julian of Norwich, Teresa of Avila, Mechthild of Magdeburg, Catherine of Norwich, Hadewijch, Therese of Lisieux, Beatrice of Nazareth, Elizabeth of the Trinity, Catherine of Genoa, Hildegard of Bingen, and more recently, Simone Weil. In general, church history and the literature of both theology and spirituality have been what one critic has termed "womanless history."

The two problems presented here are that theology and spirituality thus assume traditional masculine concepts, goals, and thought processes, and that the "normal" shape of spirituality is linear, including dualities, hierarchical organization, and ladders of success or achievement. In her book *Sex, Sin and Grace*, Judith Plaskow addresses at least two ways in which this masculine domination of the field of spiritual theology has produced an inherent bias. The first is that the sins that men are encouraged to confess, such as pride, ambition, and egotism, are qualities that should be encouraged in women who are oppressed, rather than qualities categorized as sin. The second is that the ladders of spiritual growth, so traditional to medieval piety and to the monastic rules of life, reflect stereotypically masculine concerns with security, success, and hierarchical superiority.

In short, the traditional literatures of theology and spirituality are so dominated by culturally conditioned male assumptions that they provide too narrow a range of options for men to explore either the fullness of human spiritual capacity or the richness of the godhead. These theological categories are often so removed from human experience as to be completely irrelevant to either males or females. As Emerson observed in his essay "Spiritual Laws":

> Our young people are diseased with the theological problems of original sin, origin of evil, predestination, and the like. These never presented a practical difficulty to any man—never darkened across any man's road, who did not go out of his way to seek them. These are the soul's mumps, and measles, and whooping-coughs, and those who have not caught them cannot describe their health or prescribe the cure. A simple mind will not know these enemies.

Suppression of Range of Emotions

Little boys seem at times to know only three forms of emotional reaction: elation, tears, and hitting (and one should always hit rather than be seen to cry). Prayer demands the entire range of human emotions, yet many traditional males have suppressed a significant percentage of their own emotional structure. This is why their children find men distant, cold, or distracted. It is also why men tend to express their anger in occasional explosions rather than through a less threatening moment-to-moment processing. Like the pressure mounting deep inside a volcano, the emotional build-up is often invisible until the explosion. This failure to process feelings regularly is also why men suffer disproportionately more than women from diseases that are triggered or exacerbated by emotional repression, such as ulcers, heart attacks, strokes, and gastroenteritis. According to medical studies, of the ten leading causes of death in America, nine are associated with the roles and functions traditionally assigned to men. Most violent crimes in America are committed by young men between the ages of 13 and 24, when they are busy trying to prove their manhood to themselves and to each other, for violent callousness is somehow equated with being a real man.

Men are traditionally taught not to cry, to "tough it out," to "walk like a man," to stand tall in the saddle, to keep up their defenses, and not to allow themselves to be vulnerable. No wonder women say to us again and again, "I asked you how you feel, not what you think"; no wonder so many of us are tempted to run away, for when we are asked to feel, we don't know how, since our feelings have lain dormant for so long. We men are best at think-tanking, brainstorming, being idea men or doers. Relationships in the economic marketplace are allowed only when they serve the greater good of the company, and even then they are strictly regulated in order not to get out of control or interfere with smooth operations. Like the dynamics of the corporate world, the prayers of the church tend to be formal, proper, emotionally dry, and distanced. Rules and formulae are followed in the structuring and sequential ordering of prayers, an IBM-like conformity is encouraged in the place of spontaneity, and God is addressed in the same tone and manner with which a junior employee approaches the CEO.

Further, emotions are confusing for men because one of the few times when they allow themselves to feel emotion is in the process of sexual activity. Therefore, if we feel emotions, we must be on our way to sex, but women tell us they are tired of being sexual objects for men, and anyway, sex leads to the loss of erection and therefore to the loss of drive and power in traditional male terms. Emotions scare us, and emotions confuse us. And emotions toward men are particularly taboo, because they might lead to sex with men. And emotions toward God might lead to too much intimacy.

Valuation of Self-sufficiency

I grew up with a father who, no matter how lost he was on the family vacation, would never stop at a gas station to ask for directions. Rather than admit that he could not extricate himself from his own predicament, he would spend hours in blind frustration driving around until he stumbled across the correct route. The rugged pioneer spirit of America learned to value lonely survival in the wilderness against almost insurmountable odds. The mythological frontiersman did not ask for help, was never out of control, healed his own wounds, and was ruggedly independent and self-sufficient. In the process he learned to shun relationships and interdependence, both of which threatened to undermine his survival; for once he was not alone, once he was dependent or depended on, the odds of disaster increased exponentially. Viewing the art of Western American artists such as Frederick Remington or Jo Moran, one is struck over and over by the rugged independence, the one man against the odds, the loneliness and isolation of the figures.

All this is a form of ego-centricity, an absorption in the "I" to a degree that one can no longer focus on anything else, including friendship, intimacy, or eros, all of which imply reaching outside oneself for the kind of fulfillment that is not possible through the ego alone. And so in prayer: if men do not value relationship and interdependence, they have not opened themselves to the power and healing direction of God. If men are afraid to ask for help on a family vacation, how will they ask God for help? If men are afraid to let go of the security of self-sufficiency and of hierarchical ordering, how will they make room for God to depend on them as co-creators?

Misunderstanding Relationships

Because we have been so conditioned to be independent and goal-oriented, men misunderstand the value and process of reciprocal relationships, which inhibits our sense of self in God's eyes and devalues our interdependence with creation and with the rest of humanity. The most traditional theologies and spiritualities have tended to see humankind in the role of passive recipient of God's wish and whim, as pawns in the grand design of redemption, or as lost persons whom Christ came to rescue because they were so helpless. This sort of passive receptiveness is difficult for many men to understand beyond the level of abstract theory, since men prefer to understand themselves as powerful rather than powerless. Equally foreign to some men is the idea of reciprocal relationship. Such reciprocity exists in an image of a God who self-limits in order that we might exist at all and then demands that we help God grow more fully into God-hood as we grow more fully into being human. This type of theology is sometimes referred to as the theology of friendship, and has been developed particularly by Sallie McFague and Herb Richardson.

But sociological studies of men and friendship indicate that few men have any friends at all, and when they do, whatever reciprocity exists within the relationship is based upon a dividing up of roles and responsibilities, as opposed to mutual sharing. Such studies, including the work of Jonathan Block, Michael McGill, and Lillian Rubin, indicate that men have sequential friends, each assuming specific tasks within the narrowly defined area of that friendship. Thus God could become one on a man's list of many friends: Vic is the friend I go fishing with; Tommy is the friend I carpool with; Steve is the friend I carouse with; God is the friend I discuss my spiritual life with; and Joe is the friend I talk to about my marital problems. God has a specific role as part of the sequence, but most men would prefer that their friends do not shift roles or arenas of authority within the sequence. The boss may be invited home to dinner on occasion, but he is not usually invited as well to move into the guestroom or to be more intimately related to the private details of one's life. Men's repertoire of models of intimate relationship is extremely limited, and perhaps that is why those who are doing the most significant work in the theology of friendship are women theologians. Friendship does not have goals within it and implies no task or sense of accomplishment, and so many men have trouble understanding why friendship with anyone is important, including friendship with God. Therefore playfulness is shunned—that kind of giggling, relaxed, storytelling and silly time that is a part of intimacy—and in the course of it all we lose our sense of the value of playing around with the high-spirited God.

In addition, many men have been seduced by a traditional exegesis of the Genesis creation account, particularly the combination of the word "dominance" with the gender-exclusive translation of "man." The result has been a traditional patriarchal hierarchy of natural law: Man is the head of all creation; woman is subordinate to man the head. Next in authority and worth, and hence in the eyes of God, are children, intelligent animals, dumb animals, and at the bottom is all of inanimate creation. Thus all of creation is understood as having been given by God to males for their use and exploitation. But when men get used to exploiting nonmales, the temptation is to exploit other males as well. Neither exploitation is reflective of God's love for human dignity.

Traditional interpretations of the Genesis creation account function too often today as arguments against responsible stewardship, justifying exploitation of other human beings and callousness to God's presence in the nonhuman elements of creation. St. Francis offered an alternative vision by referring to the heavens as Brother Sun and Sister Moon, as did the Native Americans who understood well their deep connection to nature. Matthew Fox, Rosemary Ruether, and other theologians have begun the systematic articulation of creation theology, reclaiming the scriptural basis for understanding humanity as one of the many equal and codependent parts of God's creation. In such a view, ecological tragedies, such as the Exxon oil spill or the rape of the rain forests, become theological tragedies, and men are called to reorder their priorities.

Not only is the concept of "dominance" to be blamed; as well we must refuse the blanket term "man." Sensitive males should be objecting violently to its generic use, for we are victimized by it in two ways. First, it assumes that something called "man," generically, is normal, and such a concentration on normalcy wipes out human individuality and uniqueness. Second, it denies the specificity of the male experience, thereby preventing us from understanding the experience and perceptions of women and thence our own experiences and perceptions both as they match and contradict women's. If all males and females are generic "man," then females are indistinguishable from males, one male is indistinguishable from the next, and none of us knows who we are. Universal terms wipe out the richness of particularities, and therefore ultimately destroy the rich intended variety of God's good creation.

Doing as Preferred
to Being

The insistence that to "do" something is categorically more manly than to "be" something, or simply "to be," is a common male temptation. As General George Patton said, "All real American men love to fight," or as one of my male seminarians said to me once, "If I'm going to be in the army [the church militant], I want to be on the front lines." In two different places in the Gospels (Mark 5:36 and 10:21; see also Luke 10:25-28, Luke 18:18, and John 6:28-29), men come to Jesus to ask him what they must do to inherit the kingdom of God. Jesus responds that they cannot get there by *doing* something; they can get there only by *being* something. In neither case do the men like Jesus' answer.

Men have long taken their sense of identity from external measures such as salary earned, goals achieved, children sired, or weight lifted. They derive their identity from outside, but not from inside. The value of instruments, gadgets, penises, and men resides in what they are good for in relation to an object or problem external to the instrument, gadget, penis, or man himself. Often driven behavior has been shaped by childhood conditions in which the only way to get a father's attention was to achieve something; success was rewarded with attention, and hence if men try hard enough, at whatever age, perhaps they will at last have earned a smile from their powerful fathers.

Prayer, however, means yielding, letting be, letting go, being open and vulnerable, and trusting that invisible answers, if there are any answers at all, are no more preferable to simply being in relationship to God. How often have we heard male television evangelists promise us that prayer generates success, money, health, wisdom, and obedience from other family members? Prayer that gets something in return is a kind of prayer that traditional men understand—prayer in the context of cause and effect or of a product correctly manufactured. But the passivity of prayer is difficult for many men because relationships, and the identity drawn from simply being who one is in relation to another, are concepts that they have too seldom experienced, do not know how to recognize, or whose worth they do not know how to value.

Confused Identity When Not in Charge

As I have already indicated, men have traditionally derived their identity from their employment, and most men define satisfactory employment as some arena in which they are in charge of someone else. Some men in the work force have gone so far in integrating women into their employment space as to be able to give orders to women, but as Anthony Astrachan's exhaustive survey shows, almost no men have yet reconciled themselves to taking orders from women. When men are not in charge they tend to lose a sense of who they are, for they have learned that their identity comes from a job well done and from being able to give orders or delegate responsibility. The sexual function of women is to receive, and in order to do that, a man must be in charge. But again, a man is not in charge in the process of prayer, and so it may be that when a man prays, he does not know who he is. Perhaps that is why we like the saying "It is more blessed to give than to receive"; it affirms our belief that the man should be on the top and gives us an additional reason to continue to devalue women who are simple receivers, rather than givers. Sam Julty points out that the traditional male role is built upon an extrapolation from the Golden Rule: "Do *unto* others; do *for* others; deny thyself; you are your tasks."

Body-Soul Dualism

Men have been taught an insensitivity to their bodies. They have learned to drive their bodies to pain and beyond (no pain, no gain), to ignore stress and physical ailments, and either to suppress their bodily needs or to think with their groin. Yet the great classics of spirituality recognize that the panoply of prayer includes a whole-body erotic integration. Brother Lawrence and John of the Cross speak of seeking comfort by suckling upon the breasts of God. Monks wrote of Christ as their lover. John Donne asserts that true chastity is available only to those who have been raped by God. The rare vocation of celibacy is premised upon a spirituality that has disciplined a healthy human sexuality, rather than a repressed or twisted sexuality, and thus all manuals of spiritual direction designed for monastics and other spiritual directors include a generous dose of frank discussion about the importance of incorporating one's sexual feelings and imagination into one's prayer life and then disciplining them. Prayer is of its nature erotic, for in prayer we seek to be at one with God, and eros is that type of love that seeks union and fulfillment in another.

This sort of integration flies in the face of the traditional Western body-soul dualism, in which the soul is prized and the body demeaned (see Peter Brown's excellent book, *The Body and Society*). Such dualism is less typical of Judaism, which includes, for example, a *berakhah* (blessing) upon leaving the toilet, and thanking God for having created humankind with orifices by which things go in and come out. It is also untypical of Hindu spirituality, which promotes the disciplined use of bodily sexual and excretory functions as a part of the advanced stages of spiritual growth. Nor has the denial of the male body always been typical of Western Christianity. Renaissance painting was acutely aware of the genitals of Jesus: paintings by Botticelli, Titian, and Bruegel portray the Virgin Mary exhibiting the genitals of the infant Jesus to the wise men; the graphic paintings by Key, Bellange, Krug, and van Heemskerck of the crucifixion show Jesus with an unmistakable erection, symbolizing resurrection.

But contemporary Western men are often uncomfortable with the relationship between their bodily and sexual urges and their spiritual growth because they have been taught that the body is annoying, vulnerable, or on the verge of wild abandon, and therefore it is to be suppressed or ignored. The doctrine of the incarnation can certainly be understood as an affirmation by God that the human body is a good thing, every square centimeter of it, and that it is something God is proud to inhabit with us, and the vehicle through which God wants us to learn to be assured of our salvation. As Mechthild of Magdeburg said in the thirteenth century, "The soul is just as safe in its body as it is in the Kingdom of Heaven."

Fear of Chaos and
Spontaneity

The need to control structurelessness by putting everything in a hierarchical order is akin to the fear of both chaos and spontaneity. Lest we have any doubt about the historical interpretation of the word "man," we need only look again at the writings of Augustine. He interprets Ps. 8:5, "Thou hast made man but a little lower than the angels," in a literalist way, so man means males. So much for the argument that man is a generic term for all humanity. According to Augustine, this biblical passage proves God's intention that the hierarchy of creation includes angels at the top, males just below the angels, and females below the males.

For Augustine, as for many men today, it is impossible to believe that creation is organized on any principle other than hierarchiality, by order of descending worth in God's eyes. Also in an Augustinian worldview, a male-identified God sits above creation and calls things into being, creating an ordered world out of nothing though always from a distance, rather than coming down into the midst of it and getting involved directly. The doctrine of the incarnation would suggest that God did come down to get involved, but somehow this is so scary to us that God must reascend into the heavens following the resurrection. To imagine God as close, intimate, and involved in the midst of creation is too frightening for the male mind (remember that the theologians who shaped these doctrines were male). When we put God back up in the distant heavens, ever transcendent and never imminent, we are more comfortable with him because he reminds us of our emotionally removed fathers. Imminence and involvement suggest that things are not ordered enough for God to go away and let them run; imminence and involvement suggest that there might be chaos and spontaneity, perhaps like a wife who orders the house remodeled without consulting her husband, or who changes the evening's social plans without checking her husband's calendar. If men appreciate anything, they appreciate order and predictability.

Incompleteness as Failure

As I have already indicated, men draw their identity from external sources such as employment, reward, and success. Some part of this is shaped by their relationships with their fathers and is buttressed by patriarchal tradition, male acculturation, and sex-role stereotyping. Men tend to back gadgets that work, sports teams that win, goals that are achieved, and programs that yield measurable results. Father's love is often more akin to respect than to love, and respect is something that is earned, not freely given. If it must be earned, it can also be taken back again. The Earl of Chesterfield once concluded a letter to his son with these words: "Adieu! and be persuaded that I shall love you extremely, while you deserve it; but not one moment longer." Robert Frost echoed the same sentiment: "You don't have to deserve your mother's love. You have to deserve your father's. He's more particular." Women's more intimate experience of human relationships suggests that things are rarely so tidy, that process matters as much as content, and that contextual thinking is as valid as linear thinking.

In general, many male egos are wrapped up in winning, and thus failure and inconclusive results lead to a shaking of any male identity that is tied so closely to accomplishment. But prayer is not tidy, and the church has always prayed, "Not my will, but thine be done," a request that men may mouth, but which they often fear. Men who say, "I want it all, I want it now, and I want it my way" have set themselves up for severe disappointment in prayer, for however much we are called into relationship and cooperation with God, it is equally true that God's ways and God's plans are not our ways and our plans.

Linearity Over Circularity

By tradition, men have hard angular bodies, and women have soft round bodies. Michaelangelo's David captures the idealized male physique in the same sense that Reubens captures the idealized female physique. But even more importantly, men are almost without exception so phallocentric that hard means success and soft means failure. One need only think about computer language, where up indicates that the instrument is ready to do its job, and down means that something dreadful has gone wrong. Ladders go up, including the ladders of spirituality; prayer goes up; when one feels great, one is up. This in turn leads to a valuation of linearity and a devaluation of both circularity and relaxation or quiet rest. A counselor told me recently that a number of young men have come to him worried that their penises are not absolutely straight when erect, and they believe somehow this is a reflection on their manliness. Linearity surely is one explanation for male homophobia as well, for to be sexually "straight" is somehow crucial to the identity as male. In the recent movie *Casualties of War*, when one man refuses to join his buddies in raping a Vietnamese girl, they threaten to rape him as a punishment for his "betrayal" of the company of men. To be a male receiver of a man's love is considered even worse than being a female receiver of a man's love. Homophobia and the devaluation of women become very wrapped up within each other.

In reality, many men experience conflict about sex, partly due to the double message we learned as children: sex is dirty, and sex should be saved for someone you love. In other words, spend your youth accumulating the worst dose of self-loathing and repression you can think of, and then dump it on the most special person in your life. But at the same time, we know eros, or desire union, and have been taught that eros means orgasm. In orgasm we are doing something; in orgasm we are at our best; in orgasm we have proven once again our ability to perform; in orgasm we for a brief moment lose control in a manner deemed okay. But when orgasm is over, we seek quickly to regain control of ourselves, and we are suddenly down, or dead; in French, orgasm is called *le petit mort*, the little death. That is why we both seek and fear eros, and we seek and fear that same erotic component in our spiritual relationship with God.

The obstacles to the development of a healthy contemporary masculine spirituality are legion. Fortunately, no one single man suffers from all of the above hindrances; as well, many men have already begun to dig their way out from under the weight of an oppressive, narrow religious heritage. The questions remain whether the new Adam can emerge at all from the dead Adam of the received faith, how men might begin the difficult climb to health, and what the future of masculine spirituality might look like.

CHAPTER • EIGHT

Praying in Circles

How then might we help men who cannot pray or who find traditional gender stereotypes to be significant stumbling blocks in their spiritual development? This is perhaps the most difficult question to answer, since so few men have come to a comfortable enough understanding of their own identity handicaps to be able quickly to move toward undoing or compensating for them. Also complicating the problem is fear of change. Like the old Adam addressing the new, we often find our traditional identities more comfortable than some unknown future identity in which we will be healthier perhaps, but different. A particularly difficult part of being new is learning to respect ourselves in a new way, as well as learning to treat those around us, both men and women, as being at least as worthy of God's attention as we are, and at least as dignified a reflection of God's majesty.

The work of consultants Carol Pierce and Bill Page may help in plotting out the parameters of our necessary change. They have tried to identify the steps by which traditional middle-class males move from violence to collegiality and shared intimacy in relationship. Pierce and Page begin at one end of a hypothetical violence-to-collegiality spectrum, suggesting successive stages by which men might move in a change of both attitude and behavior. Their book, *A Male/*

Female Continuum: Paths to Colleagueship, also suggests a parallel spectrum for women who are changing, but that parallel spectrum is not here our concern.

From Violence to Colleagueship
Rape
Coercion
Intimidation
Exclusion
Avoidance
Discounting
Devaluation
Role slots, i.e. tending to define women as wife, gal Friday,
  secretary, breeder
Paternalism
Surfacing of anger at women's demands
Defensiveness
Indiscriminate competition
Deciding to learn
Listening and asking questions
Becoming increasingly direct and nonprotective
Connecting more personally with men
Differentiating rather than stereotyping
Sharing responsibility for relationship
Discussing collusion in role stereotyping
Connecting feelings and intellect
Valuing connectedness and autonomy equally
Embracing flexible role options
Sharing reflection upon and mutual responsibility for process
  and content
Integrating both contextual and linear thinking

Fortunately, most men are not at the most primitive stage of violence against women, that is, physical rape. However, no description of the condition of American men can ignore the significantly increased incidence of domestic violence. As our society changes at an increasingly rapid pace, and as women are more and more secure in their demands for equality and justice, some men are responding to their own frustration through stepped-up physical, mental, emotional, or verbal abuse of women and of others who are different. However, the majority of American men fall naturally within that range of Pierce and Page's spectrum between intimidation and paternalism. This distribution has little to do with age, for Southern male undergraduates can be even more cruelly intimidating to women than Northern urban corporate executives. A standard reference to women by certain undergraduate men in the university where I teach is "wench," a term of dehumanization that is unfortunately looked upon by some undergraduate women there as being cute and appropriate.

But men who are responding to the women's and men's movements find themselves toward the middle of the spectrum. The first step for such men is to decide that women's demands for justice and the bankruptcy of traditional expectations of men are important enough to mandate change. Men must first own their problems and must be willing on some level to adopt the title "recovering sexist," for it is the decision to learn that fuels the changes that lie ahead. For many, the most significant initial contact with the pressures to change comes within their marriage, as women are increasingly refusing to tolerate the neglect and inequality that have caricatured American middle-class marriage. Men's initial response to women's refusal to cooperate with sex stereotypes predictably is anger and defensiveness. Feminism and similar demands for liberation are derided when the fragile male ego can stand little suggestion that it might be wrong.

But once the decision is made that something must change, and once men have decided to learn, they may begin to move through the stages of listening and asking questions and of becoming increasingly direct and nonprotective of themselves. By these steps, men are able to arrive at the stage Pierce and Page call connecting more personally with men. This is where almost all of us fail; even the men I know who have consciously spent time in men's support groups often fail, for they do not push the masculine agenda and the possibilities for growth hard enough. In fact, they do not seem to push interpersonal connectedness hard enough, even within these groups.

Pierce and Page's spectrum is not to be understood as necessarily sequential. Like Kübler-Ross's stages of grief, one moves through the spectrum at an individual pace; stages are repeated; new stages mean that old stages must be reexamined. Pierce and Page's steps from violence to collegiality can sometimes be confused with each other and lead to doubling back. For example, connecting more personally with other men can possibly lead back to the stage of excluding women altogether or avoiding them, or it can cause new forms of anger to surface. Sharing responsibility may lead to the discovery of previously unidentified role slots or devaluation. As men embrace these steps toward change, they are further frustrated by the assumption that change moves linearly or that one can progress by a sequence of isolated problems that can be fixed one at a time. Pierce and Page have designed their spectrum in order to encourage men to focus on process, rather than measurable goals and accomplishments.

Once men have taken seriously the blockages to prayer described in the previous chapter and have begun to engage the steps to collegiality with women as suggested by Pierce and Page, they are also ready to incorporate a new spiritual dimension into their lives. How is this new information we have gained about ourselves to be translated into the male relationship with God? How can men liberate their prayer lives into a new sense of richness, variety, and satisfaction?

Healing and Working toward Wholeness

In order to experience the friendship of God, we must be able to experience the friendship of others, both in giving and in receiving. Friendship means that God is free to exist in the middle of the relationship between two men, in all its vulnerability and brokenness. The wholeness of God is not found only in the male-female relationship, in spite of some pastoral theologians' claim that God's completeness exists only in the yin-yang of the female-male bond. The fullness of God is also found in many other forms of intimacy. One reflective exercise used in spiritual direction helps men gauge how ready they are for new visions. Can you imagine that we catch a glimpse of the power of God as she dwells in the midst of the friendship between two intimate and vulnerable men—men who have found a new way to define masculinity and maleness and then chosen to live fully into this new definition? How would an artist choose to render this picture? Such a meditation often opens up new horizons of prayer for the men involved.

PRAYER, IRON JOHN, AND THE WHITE SNAKE

Among the steps toward a healthier masculine spirituality is that of healing from our own wounds, as well as the wounds inherited from our fathers. Healing is a beginning, not an end; it frees us to begin to undertake the hard work. The hard work that lies ahead after the healing is, in this case, the hard work of dying—dying to the assumption that the male paradigm is the only true and correct paradigm, dying to the assumption that males have more guaranteed rights than anyone else, dying to any and all senses of superiority. It will also surely mean dying to the ways in which the Scriptures and the tradition have been interpreted in support of patriarchal interests, interpretations by which we have been so long imprisoned. But we as religious people believe in a God who liberates, even when it means using death to liberate. The liberation promised us by God includes liberation from the crippling expectations placed upon us by traditional gender roles. In Scripture, God liberates the Jewish people from Egypt into a new spiritual intimacy with God at Sinai, into a new bonding with the soil of Palestine, and into a new sense of community and interdependence.

Men now have exciting new opportunities to grow into a masculine spirituality that takes the form of a space-making, question-asking, self-disclosing ministry of mutual vulnerability, compelled by eros. Robert Bly calls this "healthy masculinity—a combination of compassion and resolve." It will mean imaging God in new ways not yet fully comfortable for men. It will mean living into eros—the passion for bonding and fulfillment through an intimate knowledge of other men and other women—without the typical male fear of losing control if we integrate eros into ourselves. It will mean choosing to reclaim voices within the spiritual tradition that our own fathers chose to silence, and as we reawaken those voices, we will have to make a new peace with all our "wounded fathers." It will mean learning to be with God, and not to do with God, by learning to be self-disclosive and vulnerable with others. It will mean learning to be as intimate with God as we have been with the closest male friend we have ever had. It will mean a new effort to form men-only prayer groups in which men learn to pray spontaneously, to touch each other tenderly and often, without fear, and to love other men in that group with a love like that between David and Jonathan, or between Jesus and the disciple whom he loved, men who prayed together as they held each other in their arms.

For the time being, some of our work will have to be done away from the presence of women, not because they are inferior, but because men must help other men to release themselves from the crippling burden of centuries of misogyny and patriarchy. A masculine spirituality must be an integral part of the new forms of bonding open to men, structureless and questioning prayer, full of tears and laughter and touch, space-making and vulnerable, and totally open to the powerful presence of God.

A hundred years ago Ralph Waldo Emerson pointed out the way that the Christian faith can inhibit the healthy development of the masculine spirit. In his essay "On Self-Reliance," Emerson expressed suspicion of those who guarded the faith by ruling out creative exploration and adaptation to particularized need. He wrote,

> If therefore a man claims to know and speak of God, and carries you backward to the phraseology of some old mouldered nation in another country, in another world, believe him not. Is the acorn better than the oak which is its fulness and completion? Is the parent better than the child into whom he has cast his ripened being? . . . Time and space are but physiological colors which the eye makes, but the soul is light; where it is, is day; where it was, is night; and history is an impertinence and an injury, if it be any thing more than a cheerful apologue or parable of my being and becoming.

Emerson's words still ring true today as a clarion call for men to fear neither change nor the stretching of boundaries. The ebb and flow of history, both its linearity and its circularity, the predictability of the sunrise, and the unpredictability of human events must speak to us as a single parable of the continuity of the old Adam and the surprise potential of the new.

The male hierarchy of organized religion and the entrenched corporate power structure often attempt to silence men who stretch the boundaries by asking difficult spiritual questions. That is why personal change is so difficult to do alone, although alone is where it usually begins. Those who are most resistant to change are always those who stand to lose the most power when the accepted structures of authority are undermined. As Episcopal priest Eugene Monick has observed, "Men who resist serious reflection on the pomposity and inflation of patriarchal assumptions of supremacy are priapic psychologically."

A man may begin his journey to change by trying to understand the woman to whom he is married, then trying to understand the institutional church, and finally trying to understand his faith. At every turn of the question, he may be discouraged from rocking the boat. Perhaps he will be accused of not being a man, for men learn to ridicule each other by denigrating the true masculinity of anyone who threatens them. Those for whom the traditional expectations have become untenable will persevere in their questioning, reminding themselves that the accepting love of Christ is both gentle and unconditional.

A dilemma of the new male spirituality is that men seek it in response to women's demands and then find their search for health blocked by other men. Pierce and Page illustrate the same point by citing the opposition of the conservative far Right to change in any area where powerful men presently make others' decisions for them: the antiabortion movement, the new focus on the traditional family, unquestioned support for militarism, the ugliness of white racism in public policy, and the fundamentalist religious upsurge. These are all signs of men reacting to the movement of women into new self-understandings, "but more importantly, it is the reaction of men towards other men who dare to move along the continuum." In other words, the failure of men to realize the new Adam can be blamed as much on other men as on themselves. Primarily through undercover power plays and exclusion, dominant men use their power in order to punish other men who choose to become collegial to women. To face this punishment from our own raises the specter of being punished as children by our fathers, and so change takes an extraordinary courage for which our life experience has not necessarily prepared us. In his essay "Other Men," John Stoltenberg writes:

> Some of us are the other men that some of us are very wary of. Some of us are the other men that some of us don't trust. Yet some of us are the other men that some of us want to be close to and hang out with. Some of us are the other men that some of us long to embrace. The

world of other men is a world in which we live behind a barrier—because we need to for safety, because we understand there is something about other men that we know we have to protect ourselves from. The world of other men is also a world in which we know we are sized up by other men and judged by other men and sometimes threatened by other men. The world of other men can be, we know, a scary and dangerous place.

Emerson, too, knew well that "It is easy in the world to live after the world's opinion; it is easy in solitude to live after our own; but the great man is he who in the midst of the crowd keeps with perfect sweetness the independence of solitude. . . . You will always find those who think they know what is your duty better than you know it." To those who seek change, courage is available within the community of changing men, and through reliance upon the powerful defense of a vulnerable God.

In prayer we learn to separate dominance from masculinity and subordinance from femininity. Dominance is learned from childhood and is accompanied by feelings of entitlement: boys are taught that they are entitled to a larger share of the pie, to the professions that earn higher incomes, to a double-standard permission to exploit others. Mark Twain quipped: "One gets large impressions in boyhood, sometimes, which he has to fight against all his life." As adults, men mask their sense of entitlement and their desire to dominate with a veneer of politeness. As our society changes, more and more people are willing to point out the hypocrisy of polite dominance, and those in power are caught off guard when some child cries out that the emperor has no clothes. Those in power imagine that their veneer of entitled authority and gentlemanliness conveys their true virtue, but in fact the vices of hierarchicalism and exploitation are increasingly visible below the surface of any system that is not built upon equality and collegiality. According to Don Sabo,

Patriarchy is a form of social hierarchy. Hierarchy breeds inequity and inequity breeds pain. To remain stable, the hierarchy must either justify the pain or explain it away. In a patriarchy, women and the masses of men are fed the cultural message that pain is inevitable and that pain enhances one's character and moral worth. This principle is expressed in Judeo-Christian beliefs. The Judeo-Christian god inflicts or permits pain, yet "the Father" is still revered and loved. Likewise, a chief disciplinarian in the patriarchal family, the father has the right to inflict pain.

To those who have the most to lose—our fathers—things seem suddenly out of control, for they can no longer "manage the rational."

Prayer as Process

Once the age of Enlightenment had wed rationality and linearity to each other, the justice and power of process was forgotten. The world became a place to manage "what exists," rather than a place to wonder. Men's deeply ingrained habit of linear thinking often makes them unaware of the processes in which they are involved. Linearity can be either horizontal (as in worldly structures of power) or vertical (as in traditional prayer), but in either case it is narrow and almost exclusively self-focused. Process, the opposite of linearity, is fluid, often circular, usually untidy, and sensitive to the larger context of which linearity is only a small part. To become aware of the processes we share with others requires not just to see how everyone else fits into the hypothetical line one can trace, but rather to think contextually and to include the needs, wants, opinions, and desires of others in the larger picture where we are an integral but equal part.

Linearity dislikes any information that blurs its lines, but the focus on process demands a personal involvement from those affected, through the nonjudgmental solicitation of information from others. As Pierce and Page point out, in a situation of colleagueship everything that happens needs to be open for discussion on a regular basis. When we speak instead of listen, we can be assured that we will not have all the information. And so it is in prayer: if prayer is primarily our speaking to God rather than listening to God, we can be sure that we have little idea of what God seeks from us, or even of who God is. A prayer relationship with God must be as collegial as the professional relationship between man and woman or between any two persons. And as in collegiality, where two people function autonomously but stay in constant close communication with each other, so in prayer we learn to function autonomously and equitably, listening to God with the same frequency and intensity that we expect God to listen to us.

The truth of God is found in the depth process of human experience rather than in the linearity of logical proofs and doctrinal formulas. Even if we name the process, it is worth nothing if it is not lived. Although we may imagine ourselves trapped in linear thinking, our lives actually function in circles, webs, ambiguities, and hazes, and since this is where our lives truly are, it is in circles, webs, ambiguities, and hazes that truth is to be found. Sexual stereotypes and expectations of normalcy are as susceptible to repeated exception as are doctrinal claims about the nature of God. Whatever else we may be with God, we are never finished, nor are we ever tidy. Those English translations that give God's name as "I Am" suggest a misleading certainty, for we in fact worship a God of surprises. As I have learned from David Hartman, it is more accurate to translate God's sacred name as "I am in the process of becoming what I will be for you tomorrow." For this reason we must speak of mosaics of relationship rather than rigid geometrical shapes. To be accurate, the diagram of interdependence with others or with God must always be a fluid mosaic of interlocking pieces that look different in each changing light like a kaleidoscope, rather than the icy sanity of neat squares and triangles.

When linearity became wed to rationality, prayer became wed to acquisition and solution, and the Calvinist assumption that material success illustrated any person's true spiritual worth grew exaggerated. In such an equation, unanswered prayer can be interpreted only as a sign of spiritual unworthiness. Yet our challenge to this simplistic equation also is not new. Emerson wrote:

> In what prayers do men allow themselves! . . . Prayer that craves a particular commodity—any thing less than all good—is vicious. Prayer is the contemplation of the facts of life from the highest point of view. . . . It is the spirit of God pronouncing his works good. But prayer as a means to effect a private end is meanness and theft. . . . Another sort of false prayers are our regrets. Discontent is the want of self-reliance; it is infirmity of will. . . . As men's prayers are a disease of the will, so are their creeds a disease of the intellect. . . . But in all unbalanced minds, the classification is idolized, passes for the end, and not for a speedily exhaustible means, so that the walls

of the system blend to their eye in the remote horizon with the walls
of the universe; the luminaries of heaven seem to them hung on the
arch their master built. . . . They do not yet perceive, that light,
unsystematic, indomitable, will break into any cabin, even into theirs.
Let them chirp awhile and call it their own. If they are honest and do
well, presently their neat new pinfold will be too strait and low, will
crack, will lean, will rot and vanish, and the immortal light, all young
and joyful, million-orbed, million-colored, will beam over the universe
as on the first morning.

The prayer of sensitive men must become one of spontaneity and
surprise, without rules or expectations; if it concentrates on anything
at all, then it must be on thanksgiving as opposed to self-serving
petition.

In prayer we must learn simply to be with God and to let go of
doing and of requesting that anything be done to or for us. What we
do or think is never as important as how it is done; the fluid phrases
of a pious mouth are no substitute for the love that flows from a secure
and questioning heart; a petition granted is worth far less than a
consanguine being absorbed at rest with divine love. In his recent
book *Toward a Male Spirituality*, John Carmody suggests some questions that might emerge for men when they learn simply to relax and
be present with God in prayer.

To accept their masculinity, in its ambiguity, Christian men hardly can
do better than to pray about it and discuss it in explicitly religious
terms. How ought their love for Christ to share their sense of being
male? What can they draw from the image of God as a father? What
does their love of women's beauty suggest about their emotional responses to God? How does the call of Christ to render justice sharpen
the challenge to be strong and do what is right?

The pondering of such questions, without desire for resolution, has
become the meat of the prayers of men seeking change.

Part of being with God is relaxing into our sexuality and allowing
its erotic character to feed the intimacy of our prayer lives. James
Nelson describes sexuality as "the primitive human longing for reunion
and communion . . . a deep human energy driving us toward bonding
and compassion." But it seems to me that this is as well a definition

of prayer. At a critical level, prayer and sexuality are inseparable. With dedication and the proper spiritual direction, men can learn to pray their way into a deeper and more intimate relationship with God and with other persons whom they love. This more creative, liberated form of masculine spirituality can be a state of grace. Nelson observes: "The realization of such grace is made more possible by our own conscious decisions. One is the decision to try to see myself through the eyes of the Divine Lover, for then I see myself as worthful and beloved. To view myself otherwise is an affront to my Creator." But I cannot see myself in a mirror unless I stand still, valuing the state of quiet relaxation more than that of a driven readiness for accomplishment and success.

In his story of the psychological import of the Priapus myth, James Wyly observes how seduced American men have become by the ideal of virile adolescence.

> In the Greek and Roman worlds in which Priapus was worshipped, this adolescent male image appears to have been a consciously cultivated, culture-wide esthetic ideal. This is not precisely the case in twentieth-century Western culture. It is true that with us the adolescent male appears as a physical ideal in some individual psyches. . . . However, on the contemporary culture-wide level, what is "worshipped" appears to be an adolescent male psyche, more than the adolescent male body of Greece and Rome.

Priapus, ever driven by the uncontrollable virility of his own erect adolescent phallus, was seen as dangerous by the classical cultures, for they understood that the urgency of a phallus is too often alleviated by making another person into a dehumanized or neutered object. In our own culture, we have been taught not to fear, but to worship the power of the phallus in the form of drive, ambition, success, accomplishment, and the maintenance of tumescence at all costs. At the same time, as Nelson so capably points out in *The Intimate Connection*, we have been taught to devalue the deflated penis, and along with it, vulnerability, tenderness, quietude, and softness, as the discussion of Robert Bly in the following chapter will show. Wyly goes on to observe that men are not propelled into therapy until they reach that crisis point at which they can no longer maintain their psycho-priapic state of inflation, that is, "a failed relationship, a lost job, decline of the physical attributes of youth, or anything else upon which they had become overdependent for their sense of importance or male identity in the world."

Wyly explains that the classic treatment of the psychological condition known as priapism, or the inability to relax one's inflated phallus, includes humiliation. No American male is free of emotional priapism; we do not tell each other the truth because we are afraid that if our secrets were to be let out, we would become powerless, impotent. However, such fear is unjustified: the opposite of priapism is not impotency, but deflation or relaxation. The opposite of pumping one's achievements full of air is to rest humbly in the awesome presence of God. The more inflated we become, the more in need we are of the humiliation that comes when we compare our capacity for intimacy with God's capacity, our powers of creation with God's, and our ability to forgive with God's. To be humble in the presence of God is to own the humiliating inadequacy of our individual grasp of reality, and then to relax into God's tenderness, which does not value our ability to perform but instead loves us for who we already are as images of God's own character. We cannot truly learn to be present with God as long as we idolize phallic power, not because the phallus is something to be ashamed of, but because it gives us a false sense of what God values in us. God values our wholeness of being rather than our aggressive dominant performance.

In addition to humbling ourselves, our natural male priapism can be controlled by befriending our given sexual identity, and particularly by befriending our penises. Pastoral theologian James Hillman points out the tragedy of the compulsive, false expectations that we foist upon our sexual performance.

> So much has been said about the penis in the last 100 years of psychology that I don't want to gild the lily. Still, we all know the strength of confidence that seems to stem from it. Gaining confidence from it seems to require giving it confidence—confiding in it, letting it confide in you. What do you want from it? use it for? expect? What does it want from you? Men need to notice its inherent requirements and whether [these requirements] really originate in the penis or derive from propaganda about what it should be feeling and doing.

Being victimized by the false propaganda about what we should be feeling and doing sexually makes us painfully aware of how short we fall of the healthy image of God in which we are created. Such propaganda makes us lose confidence when we cannot perform and drives some men to search for external solutions to an internal problem of masculine identity. An exaggerated concentration on the power of the erect phallus leads too many men on the disastrous quest for gratification through new "objects" outside of their committed relationships and ultimately leads to the loss of everything.

One does not embark upon the tragic phallic quest unless one is already missing the very wholeness that is being sought. Men's desperate phallic quest is an indication of the arid character of their spiritual lives. Clearly God's love for them in their relaxed, natural, uninflated state is not enough for them to trust; they seek the carnal love of others to fill the vacuum left by their failure to know the consuming love of God. If we were to know how much we are already loved by God and were then able to love ourselves with an equal comfortability, the phallic quest for external confirmation of our ability to perform and of our worth would be no longer necessary.

If sensitive men's search for intimacy cannot be satisfied through serial conquests, where then might it be satisfied? More and more men are turning to the community of their own gender in the search for intimacy, and within that movement religious men are turning to others like themselves to bolster their sense of intimacy with God in prayer. John Carmody speaks poignantly of his own search:

> But I myself am looking for a few good men with whom to discuss my shabby prayer, my forgetfulness of God's gifts, the relations between love and contemplation, the problems of getting religious experience into academically acceptable prose, the religious implications of my first significant appreciations of aging and thus mortality, my emotional distance from the Vatican shenanigans I read about in *The National Catholic Reporter*, and my feeling that I am a man without a country, at home neither in academics nor in my local Catholic diocese, which interests me as little as I interest it.

As more of us turn to the community of men for support, the issues of prayer and our spiritual health need to become a more integral part of our honesty with each other. To be this honest, we need to explore a new repertoire of meditations, designed to be processed aloud within the community of men.

New Spiritual Exercises
for Men

To differ and to be different are important parts of the spiritual meditations available to men who are changing. Rabbinic Judaism provides an enormous number of blessings to be recited upon seeing something new and unexpected, as well as about the continued marvel of the various components of our daily lives. Christianity has been less sensitive to the beauty of creation expressed in variety. One part of men's meditations, then, should include pondering the beauty and value of being different: what a wonder it is that God created some men heterosexual and some homosexual; that God created some men to be athletes and others artists; some with short penises and some with long penises; some who understand the mysteries of poetry and others who understand the mysteries of carburetors—in sum, that my most intimate friend can be both my alter ago and completely and joyously different from me. Surely we should rejoice just as much in the vastly different types of people as we do in the rich variety of ways to pray and respect them all equally.

Our meditations should also include imaginative exercises that stretch our sense of identity. Cooper Thompson tells of an exercise in sexual identity that he frequently uses with elementary school children. They are asked, "If you woke up tomorrow and discovered that you were the opposite sex from the one you are now, how would you and your life be different?" He and his co-workers report the following responses as being typical of boys: "If I were a girl, I'd be stupid and weak as a string"; "I would have to wear makeup, cook, be a mother, and yucky stuff like that"; "I would have to hate snakes. Everything would be miserable"; "If I were a girl, I'd kill myself." A similar exercise would be productive for men discussing their spiritual lives. "If I woke up tomorrow as a woman, how would my life be different? How would my understanding of God be different? What would I ask God for? Where would I most often see God at work in

140

my life and in the lives of others around me? How would my status and position in the church or synagogue be different, and how would that feel?"

It may be that such exercises are still too difficult for many men, for they demand parts of our imaginations that we do not often exercise. It may also be that we find them humiliating. Perhaps we find such exercises frightening, for we fear that sensitivity will make us weak, or worse, will "make" us homosexual. But we will not have begun to understand intimacy within the community of men until we can share aloud the creative nature of our prayer lives with each other. I suspect (and the experience of many men I know confirms this) that we are more reluctant to talk about our spiritual activity than about the intimate details of our sexual activity. But if I do not know your spiritual character, can I claim that I know you well?

Pierce and Page conjecture that such sharing will occur inside the community of men before it is shared with women, because the presence of women keeps men from changing. This occurs for several reasons. First, men perform for women and often hide their failures. Second, even feminists have a difficult time letting go of the stereotypes of what a man should be and think. And third, our introspective and spiritual life is badly impoverished because we have too long depended on women to do it for us. As long as women are present, we will continue to neglect responsibilities for our own development. Having women not be present will give men a chance to vent our anger at their demands, although within the community of men we must police each other so that our anger does not degenerate into misogyny. But anger in prayer is allowable, and we can explore ways in which becoming angry together will help our spirituality. Anger is healthy only when it leads to change and growth, rather than to retrenchment. We may be free to learn only insofar as we distance ourselves from women's presence and disencumber ourselves from tradition-bound relationships. These lessons may become available to us once we are freed from the ancient legacy of distrust between the sexes.

This is not to say that women will be absent from men's spiritual exercises any more than men will be absent from other men's. The exercises on difference are one place to begin to think of women as equal but quite distinct from men, with different journeys and different needs. Recognition of this difference can free men to concentrate on the masculine agenda, without confusing it with the guilt and anger that many men carry in response to feminism. It also can allow men to begin to articulate what is specifically masculine about the ways in which we pray, such as how our redeemed relationships with our fathers might enrich our mature prayer life, and what is complementary about the male experience of living among women as equals.

Men's spiritual development is not identical with women's, though many men seem to act as though it were. Men who have confused their spiritual needs with women's will find themselves pushed toward being autonomous and differentiated (the correctives to women's inherited role-stereotyping that women rightly seek in spiritual development), rather than learning to celebrate their acceptance, interdependency, and inclusivity within the masculine community. Among the subjects appropriate for men's meditation are the strength that comes from needing others and the value of shared power. As Carmody points out, "Power is not a 'pie' to be cut up, but something to share which grows and expands as we empower others." Appropriate men's meditations reflect not only on our weaknesses and the history of our exclusion of others, but also on what is good about being male and how that goodness is reinforced through deepened relationships.

Spirituality, like power, is also meant to be shared. Little could be more counterproductive for the American male than the current fad of seeking out a personal spiritual director and then working in isolation, one on one. The only appropriate model for the too-isolated and emotionally anesthetized male is group spiritual direction, in the company of others—preferably men—who will not rescue him by doing his work for him. In group spiritual direction, relationships cannot be ignored or covered up, and a new opportunity is presented for a man to recognize his vulnerability and the vulnerability of God.

A man's reflection on his own vulnerability would include his prayer concerning his mortality. Reflection on what it means to be loved as one who receives rather than takes, one who has an active interior sensitivity, whose sense of self is not dependent upon sports, or who identifies with the poor or society's "losers" leads to understanding vulnerability. Meditation on the vulnerability of God can lead men to contemplate the risk that God takes by being in covenant relationship with human beings, God's choice to be deeply connected and committed to another, God's engagement in the pathos of those who love God, the possibility that God can be hurt in relationships and yet will choose to continue to be open, giving, caring, and to love again. Too long we have mirrored a God who is remarkably like what men are taught they should be: powerful, judging, punishing, legalistic, fickle, and exclusive—in short, the God of Christian triumphalism. Meditation on the vulnerability of God opens up new understandings of the depth of God's love, and with it, our own capacity to be and to love in a different way.

Vulnerability is not possible for those who know only how to give or to take; it is possible only for those who know how to receive. Until we are vulnerable, we do not truly know God; in the same way, until we learn to receive, we cannot truly know God. The art of receiving is at least as complicated as the art of giving. For example, men have for centuries been willing to administer the sacraments to women, but even in churches that ordain women, many men cannot yet bring themselves to receive sacraments from women. Until we are secure enough that we can be "on bottom" and still be masculine, we will not be able to receive from women, sacramentally or spiritually. The refusal of so many men to receive from women is an indication of the depth of their male identity confusion. Shared spiritual journeys within the community of men must give men the chance to explore the full emotional range possible when one is a receiver—from women and from men who have already begun to change.

But the first task is to urge men to trust God enough to arrive in God's presence with an open heart. God requests many things of humanity within Scripture and tradition, but God demands only one thing: that we exhibit our response to God's freely offered love by showing up regularly to be with God. We can never know what it means to be comfortable with God until we make the initial effort to be present. We must learn to be as at home and at ease with God as we are at home with the women we love and trust. We must learn to laugh with God, to groan with God, to weep with God, and to shout with God, for these skills are the marks of a healthy, emotionally committed relationship. The God whom changing men seek might even be named "Home," which is presently available to us within the intentional community of sensitive men until the time when we are healed enough to move back into the larger community of all God's friends.

Beginning a Men's Group

Psychotherapists Louis McLeod and Bruce Pemberton have written about the genesis of a support group known as the Atlanta Men's Experience.

> The decision to lead an all-male therapy group was a logical extension of our friendship. We met at a party and spent several hours talking about ourselves, our mutual friends, and our beginning practices of psychotherapy. . . . Sitting together, we began to realize we had met in each other a man with whom we could share, trust and risk. After such an intense sharing, we were ready to play. Entering a room where people were dancing, we discovered everyone in pairs, including some women. With a little bit of wine and feeling quite safe, we began to fast-dance together. We were laughing, enjoying ourselves, and think-ing ourselves quite smart when suddenly the record changed to a slow song by Johnny Mathis. Looking at each other we knew it was a moment of truth. Finally one of us said, "What the hell!" . . . Slow-dancing with another man symbolizes many issues confronting men today: fol-lowing as well as leading, being receptive as well as active, letting go as well as being in control, facing homophobia as well as our attraction to other men, and acknowledging competitiveness as well as cooperative efforts. Our developing relationship with each other led us to speculate about the many men who yearn for a qualitatively different relationship with other men.

I'd known about the concept of men's groups for three years before I found one myself. I'd talked about being in one for two years before I could muster the nerve to trust being in one. And when I finally got involved, it was due to someone else's cry for help, which I could not ignore.

One September, a male student walked into my office, slammed the door, and with tears rolling down his cheeks said, "I've tried every way I can think of to be a husband, a father, and a man, and nothing seems to be working. You've just got to help me!" When I looked him in the face, I knew how serious he was. "Sit down, Lee," I said, "it's time for us to get to work on a project that we've both needed a long, long time."

I really didn't know where to begin, but hoped that prayer and a little common sense might get me through the dangerous beginning stages. I knew I was taking a risk: the men I most wanted to be in a group with were students, and I was a faculty member with responsibility for grading and evaluating these seminarians. But I also knew that a number of roles and manners of being would have to be set aside by each of us; perhaps this hierarchical evaluative structure could be set aside for a while as well. Everyone in the group would have to take risks, myself included. What those risks might be remained to be seen for each of us.

I knew one other man in the seminary who had been in a men's group previously, and I called him. The three of us met and put together a list of men we thought might be interested in exploring what trusting male-male friendship might look like. We decided to approach each of them individually, in confidence, to invite them to an initial meeting. We met that first night in my home, for it was important for us to meet where no one could hear. All the men were married except me and one other, and his place was too small for the eight people who agreed to come to the initial exploratory meeting. We decided to meet on the following Monday night from 8:30 to 10:30.

Half of our group was committed even before we began, but the other half wasn't sure. Even I, though committed, was a little unsure about the chemistry of the eight of us together. We had used some specific criteria in making our list: each man invited had to be someone

(a) we already knew something about,
(b) we hoped we could trust to be confidential,
(c) we liked both socially and in the classroom,
(d) who had a sense of humor,
(e) who took feminist thought seriously,
(f) who was known for his responsible attitude toward others,
(g) whose personality fit with the other men already chosen,
(h) whose sensitivity was readily perceivable.

We didn't really state these criteria out loud, but looking back, I think that if each man had not fit all eight the group would not have worked. But even so, the unknown elements were chemistry and commitment.

PRAYER, IRON JOHN, AND THE WHITE SNAKE

The first night we met together, we knew some, but not all, of the things we'd have to agree on. One was absolute confidentiality, another was trust, and another was agreeing never to miss a meeting unless it was absolutely unavoidable. One man had been in a group before. He began the meeting by explaining the rules in his former group. Then we talked about how our group was different and the sorts of promises and problems that our special situation presented. I recounted Letty Pogrebin's story [above, chap. 1] about the men's group that failed because it operated on a business, goal-oriented model, and I shared some of the insights from the reading I'd done previously in men's studies. At the end of the evening, after two hours, we asked if each man would commit to the process of being together for the year, growing together, and learning something new about the value of same-sex friendships. Each agreed that he would commit, though some seemed more enthusiastic and others more wary.

If you begin your own group, you will need to determine what sorts of rules might apply in your particular situation. Some of the rules we developed at the beginning were:

(a) No one should know about our existence outside the group itself, except for the wives of those who were married. (This closed membership rule later proved to be problematic, as I will explain.)

(b) Nothing said in the group could ever be repeated to anyone who was not in the group. All material, even the most innocent, was absolutely confidential.

(c) We would not discuss school (since we were all connected to the same academic institution and could have spent hours talking about the same "thunderstorms in a thimble" that we talked about outside the group).

(d) We would always meet in the same place. When I was out of town on business, one of the guys would have my house key, so that the group could meet in an environment it had grown to deem safe.

(e) We would meet once a week for two hours; those who wanted to stay longer than two hours could, but no one would feel compelled to.

(f) We would not set goals to accomplish as an excuse to disband.

(g) We would, whenever we could, tell the truth. No one, however, would be forced to tell anything he did not wish to share with the whole group, even if questioned.

(*h*) We would not use our time to discuss sports or "toys" (guns, computers, bikes, etc.), or to trash anyone, women in particular.

(*i*) We would each take the responsibility to protect our relationships with our wives or lovers wherever necessary, so that no one had to carry the responsibility of knowing secrets about someone else's wife.

(*j*) We would use our time, as best we could, to talk in "I" statements about feelings, disappointments, hopes, inadequacies, joys, failures, and fears—the very things many men never talk about with other men. We would talk about how our relationships with each other were developing, including how we supported and how we disappointed each other. We would talk about our pasts where they affected the way we are now.

(*k*) Each person carried the shared responsibility to keep the group on task and to keep the atmosphere as open and trusting as possible.

If I could have added two more rules, I know now they would have been:

(*l*) We would plan regular outings with each other, in addition to our weekly meetings. Sometimes those outings would include our spouses, and sometimes they would not.

(*m*) We would be braver about touching each other and about crying in front of the group.

But by the end of the first meeting, we knew we had something special going already. No one wanted to see the evening end.

During those first few weeks that followed, I found myself thinking about my men's support group. Slowly the irony dawned on me. Women need support groups, just as anyone who is oppressed does, because they need support in challenging and changing the system that oppresses them. But what did we, eight middle-aged, middle-class, educated, white males, need to be supported in? Our right to drink beer together? Our masculine jocularity? Our attempts to cope with being forty? Our confidence that our penises still worked? So then for a while I just called it "my men's group." But of course it's not mine; it's the one I belong to, in which I am an equal, but which I do not own. It's really *our* men's group. Sometimes between us we call it the Monday night gang, the group, or just "the guys." Sometimes I'd like to own it, because I've grown to need it so much, even when it doesn't work. That's when I most need to be reminded that it's *our* men's group, because I'm not in control, and it's not there to serve me but to show me how to grow into a new masculinity alongside and intertwined with other men who love me and who challenge me.

It didn't take long before we discovered how hard it is for a group of men, even when deeply committed to each other, to stay on task when it comes to talking about the issues that arose from our personal depths. Before long we knew what to call that dynamic we most easily lapsed into: "water-bugging," that is, skimming across the surface of things without ever mentioning much of any substance. In fact, the first couple of meetings we just "water-bugged"; I think we felt so good about committing ourselves to each other that we forgot to work. We met for several meetings before one member of the group took the risk of really opening up a lot of personal pain. He spoke hesitantly, and with a certain amount of obvious fear, because he was the first to dive so deep into himself in the presence of the group. The group handled it well, and once again we knew that we had made the right choice in our commitment. But the next week we water-bugged again for the whole two hours. Soon we learned that we had to watch out for a pattern. An intimate and deeply personal meeting one week tended to be followed the next week by a meeting in which nothing of any substance got raised. It seemed as though when we got too close to each other, we had to pull back the next week. We were unable to sustain for long the threat of honest verbal and emotional intimacy. We still struggle with the same problem, but at least we now know how to recognize the pattern.

We'd had the men's group going about six months, when in one long day four of the guys made private appointments to talk to me at home. One was worried about a relationship that he was afraid was competing with his marriage; one was worried about another male student's drinking; one had had a vaguely homoerotic dream; and one had begun to feel like he was choking whenever he thought about his father. I wasn't surprised by the individual problems; I've done a lot of counseling, and had heard these problems before. What did surprise me was that none of these four men seemed ready to trust the group with his problem, even after meeting together weekly for six months. We had talked at the beginning of the group about whether we could trust each other, but I can't remember if we ever answered the question then. Some of us took risks, even big risks, in what we revealed. Those risks turned out well, so I thought we'd grown to trust each other. But suddenly it seemed that we trusted each other at some initial level, but not yet at a deeper one.

One of the things we've learned to do together is to *not* talk. Sometimes near the end of a meeting, we fall silent. We have learned the beauty of those rare moments—eight men who care about each other deeply simply sitting together in a room in silence, "being." We end those moments reluctantly, but at least none of us feels the need to break the silence with idle chatter.

We share. When one of us has a birthday, his wife often bakes a cake for the men's group to share. We give each other small surprise gifts, including interesting material we run across from the men's movement, such as a tape by Robert Bly or an article about men's studies from some recent magazine. We spontaneously eat lunch together, babysit each other's children, or help with unexpected difficulties, such as when one member was hospitalized and we took turns sitting in his room with him.

Some of the men are more verbal than others. The talking is not shared equally, though even the less talkative of us listen intensely and carry away from the conversations new insights that support us. Special friendships have arisen inside the group; smaller groups of twos and threes have developed, though this seems so far to have added no problem to the group dynamic. The two single men are included with the married couples in meals and other activities, although at times—especially when we are doing a group activity that includes spouses—the single men feel that things are not quite equitable, and the isolation of being single is driven home, in spite of the love and caring of others.

The first real crisis in the group came at the end of the first academic year because we were all leaving each other for three months, but particularly because one member of the group was graduating and moving away. McLeod and Pemberton have a rule in their group that each person who plans to leave the group must return four consecutive weeks in order to say good-bye, so that the leaving can be emotionally processed by all involved. We weren't that far-sighted, but at least we did take one three-hour session to tell our brother who was moving away of the ways we had seen him grow and change over the year, to identify and affirm his many likeable qualities, and to share extended and repeated hugs. Sadly, too many of us succumbed to the temptation to make promises about seeing him again, even though we knew that with his moving to Hawaii, the chances were slim. A couple of the guys started to talk (while he was still present) about the process by which our departing member would be replaced in the group, and he even wanted to have some say in who would get chosen. But we realized quickly enough that such conversation was just another way of doing a final "project" together, perhaps to avoid some of the pain in the emotional process of parting. I'm still not sure we've learned well how to say good-bye to each other.

A crisis developed during the second year of the life of the group when we learned that certain other men in our larger university community felt excluded by the closed nature of our group's membership. By then our own group was aware of attempts elsewhere in the United States to create groups with open boundaries. In these groups any who wished could attend whenever they wished; they are expected to maintain the confidentiality of a session but are not required to come regularly to the group. We felt that making the boundaries of our own group that fluid would destroy the unusual trust we had built up among ourselves, and so we chose not to open our membership to all those interested in attending. I feel that our decision was right, though the price we paid was a certain amount of resentment from others and the accusation that we were promoting some sort of exclusive club under the guise of inclusivity.

I wish we had already learned to be even more open with each other, more trusting, and more vulnerable. I wish we had learned to talk even more openly about our prayer lives, though this seems to be a more private part of ourselves even than our sexual history. It took us a whole year and a half before we could open up even slightly about the details of our spiritual lives. We might have been able to achieve this quicker through set exercises, borrowed from other branches of the men's movement, but perhaps we are not yet ready to take the subject too far, because it rarely comes up spontaneously. We laugh about how much fun it would be to go skinny-dipping together, but we never seem to get around to it. We have learned to say "I love you" to each other without flinching, and we are beginning to learn to hug without smacking each other's back. Sometimes in a group we rub each other's shoulders, and often we stay long after the group is officially over, gently talking together and enjoying each other. We've more or less learned not to brag about ourselves, to puff up our own egos, or to fear each other out of competitiveness. Above all, we have begun to learn what it means to be a group of men in community, interdependent without threatening our primary relationships with spouse or lover. We have begun to glimpse on rare occasion the covenanted intimacy of David and Jonathan, of Jesus and his beloved friend, and we have caught a taste of the developing community of sensitive religious men who take women as seriously as they take themselves and who want the generations that follow us to be freed from the prison of stereotypical expectations.

As I complete the writing of this excursus, we are now at the end of the second year of meeting together weekly. Our group will soon disband because half of the members are graduating and moving away. The temptation to "water-bug" remains a sore issue for us. Even with two years of committed experience, we still have to work hard not to blow off our time together with shallow news and back-slapping comradery. We still have whole sessions that could just have easily taken place between a bunch of good buddies in some local bar. The trust is now present between us to do things on a different emotional level than we were raised by our families to do, but most of our daily environment pressures us back into the old ways. We are different from having been together, but the difference is precarious, and none of us will be able to maintain it without finding new communities of men in which we can to continue to grow. We move from our time together back out into a world still hostile to the new Adam. In the months ahead, the seeds of change we chose to have planted within ourselves will die if we do not continue to nurture them within ourselves and our relationships with others.

I have purposefully not written this excursus as a how-to manual in the hope of avoiding the tendency of men to teach each other by telling each other the rules. Instead, I've written a brief history of our men's group so that readers might find the courage to begin a group of their own. As I have spoken about this material around the country, men repeatedly say to me, "Oh how I wish I could have a group like that!" You can if you will but take the risk. The quest is worth every frightening bit of effort.

The Future of
Masculine Spirituality

*Iron John and
the White Snake*

In an interview published in 1987, and again in his recent book *Iron John*, Robert Bly, founding father and poet-guru of a segment of the men's movement, criticized contemporary American men as being soft. He observed:

> I see the phenomenon of what I would call the "soft male" all over the country today. Sometimes when I look out at my audiences, perhaps half the young males are what I'd call soft. They're lovely, valuable people—I like them—and they're not interested in harming the earth, or starting wars or working for corporations. There is something favorable toward life in their whole general mood and style of living. But something's wrong. Many of these men are unhappy. There's not much energy in them. They are life-preserving but not exactly life-giving. And why is it you often see these men with strong women who positively radiate energy? Here we have a finely tuned young man, ecologically superior to his father, sympathetic to the whole harmony of the universe, yet he himself has no energy to offer.

Bly, a fine poet and perceptive critic, has confused the positive quality of softness with the negative qualities of listlessness and mediocrity. He would have been correct in observing that many American men are mediocre. They are too often undereducated, undermotivated, tired, isolated, and confused. Frequently they are wounded and seek therefore to protect themselves to the point of having no social conscience and no sense of their own role in the redemption of creation. But "soft" is not the right descriptor; as yet, most men are not soft enough but rather have overlaid their heritage of masculine dysfunction with a thin veneer of social graces. Below the veneer still lies a well of anger and resentment, which when tapped produces an explosion of masculine rage. This condition is neither soft nor desirable. Rather, the contemporary American male needs to pursue a condition of softness combined with integrity and passion.

In the church, we have often sought leaders with these same softer characteristics, believing them to reflect the personality of Christ. But here again, even in the church, we have confused softness with mediocrity. All too often those called to leadership positions in the church have as their primary credential that they have offended the least number of people. This is not softness. It is a sad commentary that the church, like society, cannot recognize the combination of softness, passion, and integrity where it exists. One can be soft, pliable, flexible, pastoral, and sensitive—and still be brimming over with energy for life and for the good of one's community.

Iron John

Because Bly fails to recognize the superior values of softness and flexibility, he too quickly turns to an image of primitive savagery that he wishes to hold out as a goal for men who are changing. He adopts as his image a quasi-Jungian interpretation of an old fairy tale, entitled "Iron John," from the collection of the Brothers Grimm. (The original version is called "Iron Hans.") Through this story, he believes that men can tap into a corrective that will lead them to a healthy new identity.

Bly's recounting of "Iron John" opens in a forest near a king's castle. When hunters go into the forest, they fail to return. The local people begin to fear that part of the forest and to avoid it. One day an unknown hunter arrives at the castle, seeking an assignment from the king. When he is told about the mysterious problem in the forest, he sets out alone, taking only his dog, to see if he can uncover the source of the problem. As he wanders past a pond in the forest, a hand suddenly reaches up from below the water, grabs the dog, and drags it down below the surface. The hunter, being fond of the dog, is not willing to walk away and leave it. Instead, he returns to the castle and gathers other men with buckets. At the pond, they bail out the water bucket by bucket until they uncover at the bottom of the pond a huge man, covered with reddish hair all the way down to his feet. Since, like the biblical Esau, his hair is a rusty red, they nickname him Iron John. They capture the wild hairy man and bring him back to the castle, where he is placed in an iron cage in the courtyard.

Some time later, the eight-year-old son of the king is playing in the palace courtyard, and his golden ball accidentally rolls into the wild man's cage. The wild man grabs it, and the boy realizes that if he is going to retrieve it, he will have to go to this rusty, hairy man, who had been dying at the bottom of the pond for so long, to ask for its return. The boy does so, and the wild man agrees to give the golden ball back if the boy will find a way to open the cage. The frightened boy runs away at the first request. The wild man calls him back, makes the same request, and again the boy runs away. Finally, the third time that the wild man offers the same deal, the boy agrees, but points out that he doesn't know where the key is. The wild man tells him, "The key is under your mother's pillow." The boy runs to his mother's room while his parents are away, finds the key, and opens the cage to set the wild man free. When the wild man emerges from the cage, he starts toward the forest. The young boy shouts after him, "Please don't leave me! My parents are going to be furious when they come back." Iron John replies, "You're right; you must come with me." Hoisting the boy up on his shoulders, the two disappear into the forest. As they leave, the wild man is heard to say to the boy, "You will never see your mother and father again."

Bly interprets this fairy tale in a heavily allegorical manner. He understands that beyond the feminine side of any male lies a "deep pool," the psyche in which is submerged an ancient wild man covered with hair. Hair is symbolic of the instinctive and sexual side of the masculine character, with which contemporary American men have lost touch altogether. Bly calls this "the deep masculine." It is not to be confused with the shallow, macho, or "snowmobile" masculine, the empty veneer promoted by our culturally, militarily, and religiously inherited sex stereotypes. We do not know how long this wild man has lain hidden in the male psyche, but we do know that we will not be whole until he is liberated and befriended.

The young boy in the story is about eight years old, for according to Bly, that is the age at which we lose our childhood naivete, symbolized by the golden ball. "The ball is golden, representing light, and round, representing wholeness; like the sun, it gives off a radiant energy from inside." The "deep masculine" that lies dormant but seething within the American male is infused with the energy that Bly finds presently missing in American men, leading him to label them soft. This energy radiates and is not available through counseling with a minister or a guru, but only through personal, internal, confrontational work. Bly assumes that each man alone must make the choice to liberate his "Iron John." Such work is lonely; as in the story, the pond water that represses the wild man must be removed bucket by bucket—a long, complicated, and lonely process.

Bly also understands that the story could have ended in any number of ways (though he goes on to develop it in a very specific manner in his recent book). The wild man could have returned to the pond once he was freed, so that the split between the boy seeking wholeness and the giant representing instinct and sexuality would occur again, thus needing future repair. The boy could have chosen to take the key back to his mother, and instead of being set free himself, he could have become a minister, a professor, or a corporate executive. But instead, the first part of the fairy tale ends with the boy disappearing into the unknown on the shoulders of the giant, turning his back on his father and mother. For Bly, the more powerful parent is the mother; it is under her pillow that the key to the cage is hidden. The work of liberating ourselves from our parents, and our mothers in particular, cannot occur until they are "away from the house," that is, until they are deceased. Until then, men remain dependent on the collectivity of the family and the continuing approval of parents or parental substitutes. As Bly observes, "If you went up to your mother and said, 'I want the key so I can let the wild man out,' she'd say, 'Oh no, you just get a job' or 'Come over here and give Mommy a kiss.' "

Though Bly speaks of men's relationships with their fathers, fathers do not figure prominently in his interpretation of Iron John because, as has been pointed out elsewhere in this book, fathers are generally absent figures in our lives. This relationship vacuum is a product of an unspoken collusion on the part of both fathers and sons. Fathers do not know their sons not only because of their own forms of masculine dysfunction, but also because fathers are afraid that if their sons truly knew them, they would no longer respect them. Bly writes,

> The father is a little ashamed of his work, despite the "prestige" of working in an office. Even if he brings his son there, what can he show him? How he moves papers? Children take things physically, not mentally. If you work in an office, how can you explain how what you're doing is important, or how it differs from what the other males are doing? The German psychologist Alexander Mitscherich writes about this situation in a fine book called *Society Without the Father.* His main idea is that if the son does not understand clearly, physically what his father is doing during the year and during the day, a hole will appear in the son's perception of the father, and into the hole will rush demons. That's a law of nature; demons rush in because nature hates a vacuum. The son's mind then fills with suspicion, doubt, and a nagging fear that the father is doing evil things.

The "wounded" father, the mysteriously absent father, conspires with the disillusioned son to keep their relationship nonexistent. Hence, says Bly, the figure that men must ultimately deal with is their mothers and not their fathers. He admits that he thinks of his own father "not as someone who had deprived me of love and attention or companionship, but as someone who himself had been deprived by his mother or by the culture. The process is still going on."

With all due respect to such an important shaper of the men's movement, I am not as convinced as Bly of the existence within men of the mythical Iron John. Bly actively promotes men's making contact with the wild man within, but much of what he says about Iron John seems to be his personal obsession with a myth divorced from reality.

First of all, the instinctual sexual wild man he describes seems to be a product of the yearnings of Western culture, but not a condition categorically inherent in maleness throughout the world. Over fifty years ago, in her classic study *Sex and Temperament in Three Primitive Societies*, anthropologist Margaret Mead debunked the idea that there is any universally accepted definition of what societal roles are appropriate to men and to women. Her comparative methodology revealed complex cultures that consider cooking, housekeeping, and childcare to be the appropriate responsibility for men and other cultures that consider hunting, farming, and witchcraft to be men's tasks. As well, Simon Grolnick points out that fairy tales are the product of the interplay between personal and cultural psychology. If cultural psychology is a variable component, then there are no fairy tales with universal applications.

Second, I know many in the men's movement who have gone searching for their own Iron John and have not been able to uncover his existence. It may be that the repressed wild man within is an attractive but elusive goal only for men who have attempted to address their dysfunction in a shallower way and who have been unable to correct their personal dysfunction through their initial efforts. They may think that they failed in their quest for the new Adam because they did not find that wild man within. It is more likely that the failure is due to trying to find the new Adam alone, separated from the supportive community of men who can affirm the steps on such a difficult journey. It is even possible that they did not find the new Adam because they were looking for a wild man. Iron John and new Adam are probably mutually exclusive terms.

Third, I know many men who don't want to find a wild man within themselves, because the wild man described by Bly is confrontative and even cruel. He takes (the hunter's dog, the boy's ball) and gives only reluctantly. He creates fear in both adults and children. He exhibits no sense of creativity and appears to be absent of intellectual development or virtue. We already know from the proper feminist critique of our inheritance what damage macho self-centeredness, conformity, and anti-intellectualism can produce. Instead of seeking the wild man within, sensitive men should seek to nurture and to facilitate. Along the way, they need to articulate a distinct difference between feminine nurturing and masculine nurturing.

Bly rejects nurturing as an appropriate role for men and again appears to accuse nurturing men of being soft. Bly's critique almost has a tone of gynophobia about it. True, many of us are inexperienced at the feminine model of nurturing. But we must still not overlook the many ways in which men believe that they are nurturing and the importance of those methods as a balance to the feminine ways. In the process of seeking a more whole identity, sensitive leaders of the men's movement must not be allowed to put down nurturing as a positive value, whether for women or for men.

Recently a female student of mine was to undergo major gynecological surgery, to be followed by an extended recuperation period at home. She came to me for counseling, fearing that her husband would not know how to take care of her properly. I asked her to describe how she would take care of someone who was ill. Then I asked her to describe how she expected her husband would try to take care of her. I had to help her understand that though his methods did not match her initial expectations, she must not overlook his genuine attempt to care for her in the manner that he believed to be most loving: to leave her alone to sleep, to be away from the home taking care of the details that keep a family running, and to set priorities and to exercise his organizational skills in order to give her as much room, space, and privacy as possible. Because this is not usually a woman's way of nurturing, she did not see it as nurturing at all. My suggestion was that she recognize the power of what he was offering and then teach him to adapt his natural instincts as a nurturer to her more specific needs.

Bly also appears to promote a mythological naivete in children, as if there were some halcyon age of radiant lightness and energetic wholeness that boys enjoy up to about age eight. The adult men I know do not remember their childhood that way. However, many of us remember when our fathers stopped being physically affectionate with us at about that age, and many of us are painfully aware that society has provided us with no significant rites of passage to mark the transition from childhood to adulthood. As Sam Julty points out, "For most men the highlights of our natural processes of passage are few and less dramatic. If I had to choose three my vote would go to: our first cognitive [sic] erection, first shave, and first grey hair—none of which require any second-party intervention. In the course of the average man's lifetime they somehow lost their significance almost as quickly as their onset." But even in societies with marked rites of passage, childhood is not idealized nor seen to be any more perfect than the flawed and disappointing childhood that most of us remember.

The wild man whom Bly describes remains a rugged individualist. He exhibits very little sense of connectedness or of community. He is alone, whether under the pond or in the cage, and seems to need to be convinced to bring the young boy along with him when he disappears again into the unknown. Bly further insists that men must contact their own personal Iron John by working alone, bucket by bucket, to liberate and encounter their instinctual and sexual selves. They must even turn their backs on the collective male unconscious. This suggestion affirms the already too negative self-image of many men as loners, as one man against the odds, who distrusts and even refuses to request help. Bly is correct that we each need to learn to be individualists but we must do so within the community of men (and ultimately of men and women) not through further isolation of the already lonely.

The suspicion that Bly carries an unexamined gynophobia is again raised by his tendency to blame mothers for adult male role-dysfunction. In his interpretation, it is the mother who holds the potential for preventing the boy's encounter with Iron John. Most of the men's movement more correctly focuses on our relationships with our fathers as the true issue. Bly discussed these relationships in a less-developed manner in his analysis of the fairy tale. To claim our manhood, we must make peace with the wounded model from whom we learned—our fathers.

Much needed attention is already being paid to the way in which men do violence to women. As yet there has not been enough attention paid to the ways in which our wounded fathers unwittingly molded us to be violent men, by failing to point out to us the prevalence with which men do violence to other men. Shepherd Bliss highlights the male-male violence of Greek mythology:

> Hephaestus was the only one of the twelve Olympian gods and goddesses who worked, as a smith; he was lame. Two distinct stories tell of his laming. In one his mother, Hera, kicked him out of heaven. In the other, his father, Zeus, expelled him. So the origins of his wound are unclear. He was either father-wounded or mother-wounded. The

source of Philoctetes' wound is clear. The great military commander Odysseus abandons him on an island on the way to Troy after a snake bites him and his screaming becomes so terrible and the wound so smelly that the man can no longer stand his grief. The community of men throws him out.

World literature is full of men-wounded men in addition to Hephaestus and Philoctetes. In Egyptian mythology, the male god Set castrates Osiris. In Greek and Roman mythology, Priapus is humiliated by a male ass with whom he tries to compare the size of his erection. Zeus violently kidnaps the adolescent boy Ganymede to be his male lover. Cronus castrates his own father and eats his children. Apollo's infatuation with the handsome young Hyacinthus ends in disaster when the jealous Zephyrus kills the youth with an "errant" discus. The church father Origen turned his own violence inward, by castrating himself rather than yield to sexual temptation. Similarly Aschenbach "opts" for impotence and death rather than to address his passion for the boy Tadzio in Thomas Mann's *Death in Venice*. The healthy development of the new community of men will be hindered until we address more openly, and then ultimately work to correct, the male-male violence that is a part of our inheritance, handed down to us by father, mentors, employers, and institutional authority figures.

Bly, then, seems off-base in thinking that contemporary American men need to connect with the primitive and isolationist myths buried deep inside ourselves. Of course those myths are there, and we cannot be different until we confront and heal them. But this confrontation is only one part of the struggle to create the new Adam, and it must not be done alone, bucket by bucket. Instead, we need to do this individual work within a larger body of like-minded males, in order to keep ourselves honest. The first step then is to connect with the community of men. Such connection will be facilitated by replacing our isolation myths with stories of the value of men's working together in harmony with creation. To this end, I offer one possible alternative to Bly's Iron John story, a substitute tale that emphasizes creativity, dignity, the value of a nurturing response, and the importance of being connected to those who share with us God's good creation. Like Bly's example, it too is taken from the collection of the Brothers Grimm.

PRAYER, IRON JOHN, AND THE WHITE SNAKE

The White Snake

Once upon a time there lived a King whose wisdom was celebrated far and wide. Nothing was unknown to him, and news of even the most secret transactions seemed to reach him through the air.

Now he had one very odd habit. Every day at dinner, when the courtiers had withdrawn and he was quite alone, a trusted servant had to bring in another dish. It was always covered. Even the servant did not know what it contained, nor did anyone else, for the King never uncovered it until he was alone. This had gone on for a long time, when one day the servant who carried the dish was overcome by curiosity and carried the dish to his own room.

When he had carefully locked the door, he took the cover off the dish and saw a white snake in it. At the sight of it, he could not resist tasting it, so he cut a piece off and put it into his mouth. Hardly had he tasted it, however, when he heard a wonderful whispering of delicate voices.

He went to the window and listened, and he noticed that the whispers came from the sparrows outside. They were chattering away, telling each other all kinds of things that they had heard in the woods and fields. Eating the snake had given the servant the power of understanding the language of birds and animals.

Now it happened on this day that the Queen lost her most precious ring, and suspicion fell upon this trusted servant who roamed about everywhere. The King sent for him, and threatened that if the ring were not found by the next day, the servant would be sent to prison. In vain he protested his innocence, but he was not believed.

In his grief and anxiety he went down into the courtyard and wondered how he could get out of this difficulty. A number of ducks were lying peaceably together by a stream, stroking down their feathers with their bills, while they chattered gaily. The servant stood still to listen to them. They were telling each other of their morning's walks and experiences.

Then one of them said somewhat fretfully, "I have something lying heavy on my stomach. In my haste I swallowed the Queen's ring this morning."

The servant quickly seized it by the neck, carried it off into the kitchen, and said to the cook, "Here's a fine fat duck. You had better kill it at once."

"Yes, indeed," said the cook, weighing it in her hand. "It has spared no pains in stuffing itself. It should have been roasted long ago." So

162

she killed it and cut it open and there, sure enough, was the Queen's ring.

The servant now had no difficulty in proving his innocence. The King, to make up for his injustice, gave the servant leave to ask any favor he liked and promised him the highest post in the court which he might desire. The servant, however, declined everything except a horse and some money to travel with, as he wanted to wander about for a while to see the world.

His request being granted, he set off on his travels. One day he came to a pond, where he saw three fish caught among the reeds, gasping for breath. Although it is said that fish are mute, he understood their complaint at perishing so miserably. As he had a compassionate heart, he got off his horse and put the three captives back into the water. They wriggled in their joy, stretched up their heads above the water, and cried, "We will remember that you saved us and will reward you for it."

He rode on again, and after a time he seemed to hear a voice in the sand at his feet. He listened, and heard an ant king complain, "I wish these human beings and their animals would keep out of our way. A clumsy horse has just put its hoof down upon a number of my workers in the most heartless way."

He turned his horse into a side path, and the ant king cried, "We will remember you and reward you."

The road now ran through a forest, and he saw a pair of ravens standing by their nest, throwing out their young.

"Away with you, you gallows birds," they were saying. "We can't feed you any longer. You are old enough to look after yourselves."

The poor nestlings lay on the ground, fluttering and flapping their wings and crying: "We poor helpless children must feed ourselves, and we can't even fly! We shall die of hunger. There is nothing else for it."

The good youth dismounted, killed his own horse with his sword, and left the carcass as food for the young ravens. They hopped up to it and cried, "We will remember and reward you."

Now he had to depend upon his own legs, and after going a long way he came to a large town. There was much noise and bustle in the streets, where a man on horseback was making a proclamation.

"The King's daughter seeks a husband, but anyone who wishes to pursue her hand must accomplish a difficult task. If he does not bring it to a successful outcome, he will forfeit his life." Many had already attempted this task, but they had risked their lives in vain.

When the youth saw the Princess, he was so smitten with her that he forgot all danger, at once sought an audience with the King, and announced himself as a potential suitor.

He was immediately led out to the seashore, and a golden ring was thrown into the water before his eyes. Then the King ordered him to fetch it out from the depths of the sea, adding, "If you come to land without it, you will be thrown back every time until you perish in the waves."

Everyone pitied the handsome youth, but they had to go and leave him standing solitary on the seashore.

He was pondering over what he should do when all at once he saw three fishes swimming towards him. They were none other than the very ones whose lives he had saved. The middle one carried a mussel shell in its mouth, which it laid on the sand at the feet of the youth. When he picked it up and opened it, there lay the ring.

Full of joy, he took it to the King, expecting that he would be given the promised reward. The self-confident Princess, however, when she heard that he was not her equal, despised him and demanded that he should perform yet another task. So she went into the garden herself, and strewed ten sacks of millet seeds among the grass.

"He must pick up every one of the seeds before the sun rises tomorrow morning," said she. "Not even a grain must be missing."

The youth sat miserably in the garden, wondering how it could possibly be done. But as he could not think of a plan, he remained, sadly waiting for the dawn which would bring death to him.

When the first sunbeams fell on the garden, he saw the ten sacks full to the top, and not a grain was missing. The ant king had come in the night with thousands and thousands of his ants, and the grateful creatures had picked up the millet and filled the sacks.

The Princess came into the garden herself, and saw with amazement that the youth had completed the task.

But still she could not control her doubts, and she said, "Even if he has accomplished these two tasks, he shall not become my husband until he brings me an apple from the tree of life."

The youth had no idea where to find the tree of life. He started off, however, intending to walk as far as his legs would carry him, but he had no hope of finding it.

One night, after he had traveled through three kingdoms, he was passing through a great forest, and he lay down under a tree to sleep. He heard a rustling among the branches, and a golden apple fell into his hand.

At the same time three ravens flew down and perched on his knee, and said, "We are the young ravens you saved from death. When we grew big and heard that you were looking for the golden apple, we flew across the sea to the end of the world, where the tree of life stands, and brought you this apple."

The youth, delighted, started on his homeward journey and took the golden apple to the beautiful Princess, who had now no further excuse to offer.

They divided the apple of life and ate it together, and then her heart was filled with love for him, as was his for her, and they lived happily together to a ripe old age.

Why is this story of special interest as a mythical model for sensitive men? The white snake symbolizes the flaccid adult penis (flaccidity being the normal male condition) as opposed to the erect phallus. When the young servant has come to terms with his relaxed and natural masculine identity as a spiritual person, he finds that he has been given a mature wisdom, which in turn empowers him to encounter and engage the powerful mysteries of creation. Setting off in search of broadened personal experience, he refuses the successful trappings of the world that are offered to him (favors, and the highest post in the court), choosing only a horse and a small allowance, or opportunity and a modest security. Humility and adventuresomeness are the virtues that open for him the possibility of eventual health.

In the process of his encounter with creation, he befriends and is befriended by other creatures; he develops a community of relationships. He exhibits compassion rather than pride, and he interrupts his own quest in order to meet the needs of creatures in trouble. Ultimately it is this investment in relationships that offers answers to his various problems and brings the story to a satisfactory resolution. He does not solve his own problems, but the cooperative efforts of his community of support offer him solutions. Even the story's resolution is acceptable in our time: we are not told that the Princess (who has been singularly clear about her right to make her own choices) and the adventurous servant marry, but simply that they dine well and live together until they are old. The King in this story symbolizes what we now recognize as traditional masculine values—the assumptions that if he offers other people material rewards they will be gratefully received, and that if he makes women's choices for them, they will acquiesce.

The values represented in this story have too often been lost to contemporary men and to American institutional religion. The spiritual tradition speaks highly of the virtues of modesty, humility, and connectedness to community, but little that we practice conforms to what we so glibly preach. It may be that we cannot engage the higher virtues because we have not taken the initial step that the servant took: befriending his own relaxed natural masculine sexual character. If the above virtues are the result of a disciplined life of prayer, and if prayer and spirituality are inseparable because they both desire union with God, then prayer alone accomplishes for us only half the package. Our prayer is disembodied, and thus pretentious, if it is isolated from our sexuality and from our dependence upon our own gender-community.

Birth of the New Adam

New Adam waits within, struggling to emerge, struggling to be born, but the labor is long and arduous. His creation is new in that it is a renewal of who we already are. The first Adam of independence and technology is on his way to the second Adam in the fullness of interdependence and mutuality. A commitment to interdependence carries with it the promise of wholeness and the redemption of our broken masculine selves. But unless we construct these new relationships carefully, we run the risk of merely repeating the corrupt patterns that we men have traditionally mistaken for relationships. The biblical narrative confronts us with the dangers of our masculine heritage: the callous manipulation and fatal competition that marked David's "relationship" with his children; the emotional silence and the failure of nerve that typified Abraham's "relationship" with Ishmael; the accusatory mistrust by which Saul ultimately destroyed his own son's hope for happiness and commitment.

New Adam is birthed in community, but not in isolation. He is birthed among groups of sensitive men who are not afraid to sing, to tell stories, to sit together in silence, and to nurture. New Adam is birthed within communities of men who are no longer willing to settle for friendships of utility or friendships of pleasure, but who seek the deepest and most intimate levels of commitment to each other. New Adam is birthed among companions in emotion and spirituality who seek together a way to be masculine without perpetuating violence either toward women or toward men. These companions are more concerned with relationship roles than with rules and with connectedness and process than with isolation and accomplishment. These companions are liberated by their relationships with fathers and sons, rather than imprisoned by their cultural heritage of male dominance and power.

Christian men may not find easy answers within our extant spiritual heritage about what the new relationships of men-committed-inside-community might look like, but they have a clear indication of the values these new commitments will reflect: compassion, integrity, flexibility, humility, mercy, pacifism, patience, fidelity, generosity, cooperation, intellectual honesty, and dependence on others who are also within the new community of men. Above all, these relationships reflect the refusal to fear that tomorrow we will be for ourselves and others what we are already becoming today.

Like the adventurous servant in *The White Snake*, men who are changing have brave new worlds available to them, even if they are only modestly armed with opportunity and a basic sense of sustenance. The new Adam has slowly begun to emerge, unfolding from the old. Like the tight bud of a flower, we cannot see what he will look like, although we have a hint of his basic characteristics. We shall never become fully new unless we risk breaking the narrow boundaries of traditional spiritual and religious expectations and learn instead to dance, to laugh, and to lean on both our fathers and our sons in the spirited community of changing men who seek to mirror more truly the full image of God.

Bibliography

Resources in Men's Studies

Abbott, Franklin, ed. *New Men, New Minds: Breaking Male Tradition.* Freedom, Calif.: Crossing, 1987.

Ashbrook, James B. "Ways of Knowing God: Gender and the Brain." *The Christian Century* (January 4–11, 1989): 14–15.

Astrachan, Anthony. *How Men Feel: Their Response to Women's Demands for Equality and Power.* Garden City: Doubleday, 1986.

Block, Jonathan. *Friendship: How to Give It, How to Get It.* New York: Macmillan, 1980.

Bly, Robert. *Iron John: A Book about Men.* Reading, Mass.: Addison-Wesley, 1990.

Bolen, Jean Shinoda. *Gods in Everyman: A New Psychology of Men's Lives and Loves.* San Francisco: Harper and Row, 1989.

Brod, Harry, ed. *A Mensch Among Men: Explorations in Jewish Masculinity.* Freedom, Calif.: Crossing, 1988.

Carmody, John. *Toward a Male Spirituality.* Mystic, Conn.: Twenty-Third Publications, 1989.

Conrad, Peter, and Joseph Schneider. *Deviance and Medicalization: From Badness to Sickness.* St. Louis: C. V. Mosby, 1980.

Culbertson, Philip. "Explaining Men." *St. Luke's Journal of Theology* 22 (December 1988), 43–53.

168

BIBLIOGRAPHY

Doyle, James A. *The Male Experience*. 2d ed. Dubuque, Iowa: Wm. C. Brown Publishers, 1989.

Farrell, Warren. *Why Men Are the Way They Are*. New York: McGraw-Hill, 1986.

Francke, Linda Bird. "The Sons of Divorce." *New York Times Magazine* (May 22, 1983), 40–41, 54–57.

Gallagher, Winifred. "II. Sex and Hormones." *The Atlantic Monthly* (March 1988), 77–82.

Gerzon, Mark. *A Choice of Heroes: The Changing Faces of American Manhood*. Boston: Houghton Mifflin, 1982.

Gilmore, David. *Manhood in the Making*. New Haven: Yale University Press, 1990.

Goldberg, Herb. *The Hazards of Being Male: Surviving the Myth of Masculine Privilege*. New York: New American Library, 1976.

———. *The Inner Male: Overcoming Roadblocks to Intimacy*. New York: New American Library, 1987.

Gray, Elizabeth Dodson. *Patriarchy as a Conceptual Trap*. Wellesley, Mass.: Roundtable, 1982.

Hall, Roberta L. *Male-Female Differences: A Biocultural Perspective*. New York: Praeger, 1985.

Herzfeld, Michael. *The Poetics of Manhood: Content and Identity in a Cretan Mountain Village*. Princeton: Princeton University Press, 1985.

Hillman, James. "The Wildman in the Cage: Comment." In Abbott, ed., *New Men, New Minds*.

Holmberg, Fred Benton. *Touching*. Brattleboro, Vt.: Stephen Greene, 1973.

Hunter, Mic. *Abused Boys: The Neglected Victims of Sexual Abuse*. Lexington, Mass.: Lexington Books, 1990.

Johnson, Robert. *He: Understanding Masculine Psychology*. New York: Harper and Row, 1974.

Julty, Sam. "Men and Their Health—A Strained Alliance." In Abbott, ed., *New Men, New Minds*.

Klein, Edward, and Don Erickson, eds. *About Men: Reflections on the Male Experience*. New York: Poseidon, 1987.

Lee, John. *The Flying Boy: Healing the Wounded Man*. Austin, Tex.: New Men's Press, 1987.

BIBLIOGRAPHY

Levinson, Daniel J., with Charlotte N. Darrow, Edward B. Klein, Maria H. Levinson, and Braston McKee. *The Seasons of a Man's Life*. New York: Ballantine, 1978.

Lewes, Kenneth. *The Psychoanalytic Theory of Male Homosexuality*. New York: Simon and Schuster, 1988.

Longwood, Merle. "Male Sexuality: Moving Beyond the Myths." *The Christian Century* (April 13, 1988), 363–65.

McGill, Michael E. *The McGill Report on Male Intimacy*. New York: Harper and Row, 1985.

McLeod, Louis W., and Bruce K. Pemberton. "Men Together in Group Therapy." In Abbott, ed., *New Men, New Minds*.

Meth, Richard, and Robert Pasick. *Men in Therapy: The Challenge of Change*. New York: Guilford, 1990.

Money, John. *Gay, Straight, and In-Between: The Sexology of Erotic Orientation*. New York: Oxford, 1988.

Monick, Eugene. *Phallos: Sacred Image of the Masculine*. Toronto: Inner City Books, 1987.

Moyers, Bill. "A Gathering of Men, with Bill Moyers and Robert Bly." Audiotape transcript, show #BMSP-3, January 8, 1990. New York: Public Affairs Television, Inc., 1990.

Myers, Michael F. *Men and Divorce*. New York: Guilford, 1989.

Nelson, James. *Between Two Gardens: Reflections on Sexuality and Religious Experience*. New York: Pilgrim, 1983.

———. "Reuniting Sexuality and Spirituality." *The Christian Century* (February 25, 1987), 187–90.

———. *The Intimate Connection: Male Sexuality, Masculine Spirituality*. Philadelphia: Westminster, 1988.

Off Their Backs . . . and on our own two feet. Anonymous. Philadelphia: New Society Publishers, 1983.

Osherson, Samuel. *Finding Our Fathers: The Unfinished Business of Manhood*. New York: Free Press, 1986.

Pierce, Carol, and Bill Page. *A Male/Female Continuum: Paths to Colleagueship*. Laconia, N. H.: New Dynamics, 1986.

Plaskow, Judith. "Divine Conversations." *Tikkun* 4 (1990): 18–20, 85–88.

Pogrebin, Letty Cottin. *Among Friends: Who We Like, Why We Like Them, and What We Do with Them*. New York: McGraw-Hill, 1987.

BIBLIOGRAPHY

Raphael, Ray. *The Men from the Boys: Rites of Passage in Male America.* Lincoln: University of Nebraska Press, 1988.

Rhodes, Sonya, and Marlin Potash. *Cold Feet: Why Men Don't Commit.* New York: E. P. Dutton, 1988.

Rubin, Lillian B. *Intimate Strangers: Men and Women Together.* New York: Harpers, 1983.

Sabo, Don. "Pigskin, Patriarchy and Pain." In Abbott, ed., *New Men, New Minds.*

Sanford, John A., and George Lough. *What Men Are Like: The Psychology of Men, for Men and Women Who Live with Them.* New York: Paulist, 1988.

Seidler, Victor J. *Rediscovering Masculinity: Reason, Language and Sexuality.* London and New York: Routledge, 1989.

Silber, Sherman J. *The Male from Intimacy to Old Age.* New York: Charles Scribner's Sons, 1981.

Steinmann, Anne, and David J. Fox. *The Male Dilemma.* New York: Jason Aronson, 1983.

Stoltenberg, John. "Other Men." In Abbott, ed., *New Men, New Minds.*

Tevlin, Jon. "Of Hawks and Men: A Weekend in the Male Wilderness." *Utne Reader* (November/December 1989), 50–59.

Thompson, Cooper. "A New Vision of Masculinity." In Abbott, ed., *New Men, New Minds.*

Thompson, Keith. "What Men Really Want: A New Age Interview with Robert Bly." *New Age* (May 1982), 30–37, 50–51.

Viorst, Judith. *Necessary Losses: The Loves, Illusions, Dependencies and Impossible Expectations That All of Us Have to Give Up in Order to Grow.* New York: Simon and Schuster, 1986.

Witkin-Lanoil, Georgia. *The Male Stress Syndrome: How to Recognize and Live with It.* New York: Newmarket, 1986.

Wyly, James. *The Phallic Quest: Priapus and Masculine Inflation.* Toronto: Inner City Books, 1989.

Additional Resources Consulted

Aelred, Saint. "Spiritual Friendship." In Bernard of Clairvaux, *The Love of God.* Edited by James M. Houston. Portland: Multnomah, 1983.

BIBLIOGRAPHY

Agnon, Shemuel Yosef. *Days of Awe.* 7th ed. Jerusalem: Schocken Books, 1972.

Aristotle. *The Nicomachean Ethics.* Translated by H. Rackham. Loeb Classical Library. London: William Heinemann Ltd, 1934.

Bettelheim, Bruno. *The Uses of Enchantment: The Meaning and Importance of Fairy Tales.* New York: Random House, 1977.

Brown, Peter. *The Body and Society: Men, Women and Sexual Renunciation in Early Christianity.* New York: Columbia University Press, 1988.

Brown, Rita Mae. *Rubyfruit Jungle.* New York: Bantam, 1988.

Buber, Martin. *Eclipse of God: Studies in the Relation between Religion and Philosophy.* New York: Harper, 1952.

———. *I and Thou.* 2d ed. New York: Charles Scribner's Sons, 1958.

———. *Between Man and Man.* New York: Collier, 1965.

Büchler, Abraham. *Studies in Sin and Atonement in the Rabbinic Literature of the First Century.* New York: Ktav, 1967.

Carden, John, ed. *Another Day: Prayers of the Human Family.* London: Triangle/SPCK, 1986.

Chakham, Amos, ed. *Sepher Yishayahu.* The Daat Miqra series. Jerusalem: Mossad HaRav Kook, 1984.

Culbertson, Philip, and Arthur Shippee. *The Pastor: Readings from the Patristic Period.* Minneapolis: Fortress Press, 1990.

Daube, David. *Studies in Biblical Law.* New York: Ktav, 1969.

Diogenes Laertius. *Lives of Eminent Philosophers.* Vol. 2. Translated by R. D. Hicks. Loeb Classical Library. London: William Heinemann Ltd, 1925.

Dubois, Marcel. "What a Christian May Expect from Reading the Hebrew Bible." *Christian News From Israel* 24 (Spring 1974): 170–74.

Dyson, Freeman. *Infinite in All Directions.* New York: Harper and Row, 1988.

Eliade, Mircea. *Rites and Symbols of Initiation: The Mysteries of Birth and Rebirth.* Translated by Willard R. Trask. New York: Harper, 1958.

Emerson, Ralph Waldo. *Essays: First and Second Series.* New York: First Vintage Books, 1990. See especially the essays "On Self-Reliance" and "On Friendship."

BIBLIOGRAPHY

Freud, Sigmund. *The Standard Edition of the Complete Psychological Works of Sigmund Freud*. Translated by James Strachey. 23 vols. and supp. London: Hogarth, 1963. See especially "Analysis Terminable and Interminable" in Vol. 23.

Friedlander, Gerald, trans. *Pirkei de Rabbi Eliezer*. New York: Sepher-Hermon, 1916.

Friedman, Edwin. *Generation to Generation: Family Process in Church and Synagogue*. New York: Guilford, 1985.

Fromm, Erich. *Man for Himself: An Inquiry into the Psychology of Ethics*. New York: Rinehart, 1947.

Gibran, Kahlil. *The Prophet*. New York: Alfred A. Knopf, 1988.

Goldin, Judah, trans. *The Fathers According to Rabbi Nathan*. New York: Schocken Books, 1955.

————. *The Living Talmud: The Wisdom of the Fathers*. New York: New American Library, 1957.

Gotthold, Zev. "Baptism." *Christian News from Israel* 26 (Spring 1977): 77–80.

Gotthold, Zev. "How to Remember the Exodus from Egypt" (in Hebrew). *Mahanayim* 44 (Nisan 1960), 94–102.

Graves, Robert. *The Greek Myths*. 2 vols. Baltimore: Penguin, 1955.

Grolnick, Simon A. "Fairy Tales and Psychotherapy." In *Fairy Tales and Society: Illusion, Allusion and Paradigm*. Edited by Ruth B. Bottigheimer. Philadelphia: University of Pennsylvania Press, 1986.

Harrisville, R. A. "The Concept of Newness in the New Testament." *Journal of Biblical Literature* 74 (1955): 69–79.

Hartman, David. *Joy and Responsibility: Israel, Modernity and the Renewal of Judaism*. Jerusalem: Ben-Zvi Posner, 1978.

Herberg, Will. *Judaism and Modern Man: An Interpretation of Jewish Religion*. New York: Farrar Straus and Young, 1951.

Herberg, Will, ed. *The Writings of Martin Buber*. New York: Meridian Books, 1956.

Herman, Gabriel. *Ritualised Friendship and the Greek City*. Cambridge: Cambridge University Press, 1987.

Higger, Michael. "Pirkei de Rabbi Eliezer." *Horev* 10:19-20, Elul, 1948.

BIBLIOGRAPHY

James, William. *The Varieties of Religious Experience: A Study in Human Nature.* Cambridge: Harvard University Press, 1985.

Kehati, Pinhas, ed. *Mishnayot.* 9th ed. Vol. Nezikin I, Baba Metzia. Jerusalem: Heichal Shelomo, 1977.

Klebsch, William A., and Charles R. Jaekle. *Pastoral Care in Historical Perspective.* Englewood Cliffs, N.J.: Prentice-Hall, 1964.

Maimonides, Moses. *The Guide of the Perplexed.* Translated by Shelomo Pines. Chicago: University of Chicago Press, 1963.

———. *Commentary on Pirkey Avoth.* Edited by Paul Forchheimer. New York: Feldheim, 1983.

Malherbe, Abraham J. *Moral Exhortation: A Greco-Roman Sourcebook.* Philadelphia: Westminster, 1986.

Mandelbaum, Bernard, ed. *Pesikta deRav Kahana.* 2d augmented ed. New York: Jewish Theological Seminary, 1987.

Mead, Margaret. *Sex and Temperament in Three Primitive Societies.* New York: William Morrow, 1963.

Neher, Andre. *The Exile of the Word, from the Silence of the Bible to the Silence of Auschwitz.* Translated by David Maisel. Philadelphia: Jewish Publication Society, 1981.

Niebuhr, Reinhold. *The Nature and Destiny of Man: A Christian Interpretation.* New York: Charles Scribners' Sons, 1941.

Nock, Arthur Darby. *Conversion.* London: Clarendon, 1969.

Piercy, Marge. *To Be of Use.* Garden City, N.Y.: Doubleday, 1973.

Plaskow, Judith. *Sex, Sin and Grace: Women's Experience and the Theologies of Reinhold Niebuhr and Paul Tillich.* Lanham: University Press of America, 1980.

Plato. *Lysis, Symposium, Gorgias.* Translated by W. R. M. Lamb. Loeb Classical Library. London: William Heinemann Ltd, 1932.

Plutarch. *Moralia.* Vol. 2, trans. by Frank Cole Babbitt; Vol. 9, trans. by Edwin Minar, F. H. Sandback, and W. C. Helmbold; Vol. 10, trans. by Harold North Fowler. Loeb Classical Library. London: William Heinemann Ltd., 1928–61.

Pritchard, James B., ed. *Ancient Near Eastern Texts Relating to the Old Testament.* Princeton: Princeton University Press, 1950.

Pritchett, Jim. "The Essential Nature of Humanity and the Individual's Ability to Change: The Views of Freud and Fromm and the Implications of Those Views for the Christian Pastoral Care Giver." Unpublished paper, Sewanee, Tenn., 1990.

BIBLIOGRAPHY

Ricklin, F. *Wish Fulfillment and Symbolism in Fairy Tales*. New York: The Nervous and Mental Disease Publishing Company, 1915. Reprint. New York: Johnson Reprint Corporation, n.d.

Schüssler Fiorenza, Elisabeth. *In Memory of Her: A Feminist Theological Reconstruction of Christian Origins*. New York: Crossroad, 1983.

Schwartz, E. "A Psychoanalytic Study of the Fairy Tale." *American Journal of Psychotherapy* 10 (1956): 740–62.

Silbermann, A. M., ed. *Chumash with Targum Onkelos, Haphtoroth and Rashi's Commentary*. 5 vols. Jerusalem: Silbermann Family, 1934.

Soloveitchik, Joseph. "Lonely Man of Faith." In *Studies in Judaica in Honor of Dr. Samuel Belkin*. Edited by Leon D. Stitskin. New York: Ktav, 1974. (First published in *Tradition* 7 [1965].)

Steinberg, Leo. *The Sexuality of Christ in Renaissance Art and in Modern Oblivion*. New York: Pantheon, 1983.

Torer, Haim ben Shelomo. *Derashot al Inyyanei Shabbat al pi Pardes*. Mohilov, 1813.

Trible, Phyllis. *God and the Rhetoric of Sexuality*. Philadelphia: Fortress, 1978.

———. *Texts of Terror: Literary-Feminist Readings of Biblical Narratives*. Philadelphia: Fortress Press, 1984.

Urbach, Ephraim E. *The Sages: Their Concepts and Beliefs*. 2 vols. Jerusalem: Magnes Press (Hebrew University), 1979.

Weber, Eugen. "Fairies and Hard Facts: The Reality of Folktales." *Journal of the History of Ideas* 42 (1981): 93–113.

Wolfson, Harry Austryn. *Philo: Foundations of Religious Philosophy in Judaism, Christianity and Islam*. Cambridge: Harvard University Press, 1947.

Ysaebaert, J. *Greek Baptismal Terminology: Its Origins and Early Development*. Nijmegen: Dekker and Van de Vegt, 1962.